THE JOY
OF PASTA

THE JOY OF PASTA

SIMAC'S CUISINE COLLECTION

Graphic project and editorial coordination by
Simonetta de Nisco

All recipes have been worked out and tried by
Amica SIMAC

Photographs by Adamo Photographer, set and taken
at the Restaurant of "Hotel Adda" in Paderno
d'Adda

Drawings by Salvatore Cibelli

Flatware and glasses by Picowa (Milan)

Pots and pans by Italinox

Paintings by Mario Jetti

Masks by Romualdo Priore

Cover: Continental Pubblicità

Advertising consultant: Ubaldo Galli

Translation by Fulvia Dassi

Supervision of the English version by Sherry Livingston
and Elisa Celli - food and wine writer

Fresh pasta: a brief history

The word "pasta" comes from the late Latin, which is derived from ancient Greek "pástē", a word used to designate a sort of porridge. The oldest kinds of pasta we know of are "lasani", from the Greek "lasanon", which were already known by the Etruscans and by the inhabitants of some Italian regions. The "lasani" was a sort of pasta to be cooked with broth and similar in shape to the present "lasagne".

Also "maccheroni", whose name derives possibly from the Greek "makrós" (long) or "makārios" (blessed) were to be cooked with broth and they were, therefore, "the food, which blesses", or "the God's food". Yet, this word referred likely to a kind of pasta, made mainly of flour, served in the ancient times at funeral banquets to honor the dead, hence, the blessed ones.

The Greek colonists, who emigrated to near lands to search for a new homeland and above all for new land to cultivate, took the typical dishes of their country as well as their customs with them. Maccheroni, therefore, came to the Greek colony of Naples, where this pasta was adopted as the local, favorite dish. Yet, the Neapolitans boast they have "invented" maccheroni and support this claim with curious legends. Their being so likeable along with their imagination, creativity and their strong local pride have such a great convincing power that many people give credit to them for being "the inventors of maccheroni". This is also due to the fact that they have contributed decisively to the triumph of maccheroni thanks to a truly Neapolitan invention, "pummarola", a tomato sauce made with the new vegetable, which, after the discovery of the New World, had been taken to Europe and found its natural "habitat" in Southern Italy, in the area around Naples.

One has to go back as far as the mid-XIIth century to find "vermicelli" quoted in Arab text! Vermicelli had already become so popular under the name of "Itriya" that they were exported from the area of Palermo in Sicily, where they were manufactured, up to the Italian regions of Campania and Apulia.

As a matter of fact, the word still exists in the Sicilian dialect: "tria", refers to the wooden press, used to make "vermicelli" by hand, and more generically to the pasta obtained with the use of the press itself. Then, how does it come that many eminent texts point to China as the homeland of "vermicelli"? This is due most likely to a mere coincidence, unless we want to imagine the fascinating adventures of some European wayfarers, who would have gone as far as that remote land.

On the other hand, we know of some pasta, made of wheat and bean in addition to that made of rice flour being eaten in China in the ancient times. In his book "Milione", Marco Polo reports on a thread-like shaped food, made of rice and soybean flour, which the Chinese cooked and was supported-attributing the invention of "vermicelli" to the Chinese.

Pasta has been quoted also by the Italian writer Boccaccio, who tells of how "Niuna altra cosa facevan che far maccheroni e raviuoli e cuocerli in brodo di capponi..." (they didn't do anything but make maccheroni and ravioli and they cooked them with capon broth) in one of his short stories. We also know that one day Maria de Medici (1573-1642) went into a tavern in Paris and the Italian cook served her some hot maccheroni. Pasta in its various shapes was, therefore, a well known food, which, nevertheless, the upper class only could afford because its preparation was quite complex.

Pasta became a popular dish for almost everyone only when the first machines to prepare it at home spread out. The dough was kneaded by hand and the press shaped the pasta, which was then hung outdoors on ropes stretched under porches or on the balconies to dry. So pasta, which dried under the sun, was like the flag of an eating tradition, which was growing stronger and stronger.

The first semi-automatic machines to produce pasta appeared first at the beginning of the 1800's and the most famous centers for pasta production were in Naples. The industrial production of pasta began there with the new machines, and around 1830 with the "kneading machines". In the 1870's the first hydraulic presses and mechanical kneaders were introduced and they limited man's work to machine monitoring and to manual operations. In 1875 the first plants for the artificial drying process were improved; leading to the hot air plant built at the De Cecco factory at Fara S. Martino, near the town of Chieti. All the other regions, which had an extremely well-established tradition for pasta-namely Liguria, Sicily and Emilia - specialized in different kinds of pasta according to their ancient customs.

The first real, perfectly automated, full-cycle pasta machine was built in 1933 thanks to the invention of the Fratelli Braibanti Company, Italian pasta manufacturers. A new era began for pasta, whose first signs had already been clear, when the Italian pasta manufacturers had emigrated, spreading their art all over the world. Several pasta factories were built abroad, but Italian pasta still ranks first; Italian industry exports its products to every country and millions of tons of pasta are consumed in America every year, with the number increasing. This is the "Era of Pasta"; pasta has become 'chic' - 'the health food' - 'the new diet food' - 'the great economical food' - 'the fun food' - and 'the food with many variations' - classical recipes and creative recipes. "Make your own pasta as you like...to your choice...enjoy and good health".

"Custom-made" pasta

"Il est essentiel qu'il soit cuit seulement au moment d'être employé. Un macaroni réchauffé ne peut jamais donner qu'un mauvais résultat".

A. Escoffier - "Le Guide Culinaire".

Pellegrino Artusi, famous gastronome and author of "La scienza in cucina e l'arte di mangiar bene", wrote about green tagliatelle: "...il bello di tali paste è la loro lunghezza il che indica l'abilità di chi le fece" (the nicest thing of this kind of pasta is its length, which shows the skill of that who made it). Such manual skills have gradually disappeared in a century's span of time. This is actually a pity because fresh, homemade pasta is good, genuine, cheap and has a high nutritional value; and everybody loves it! Pasta is the Italian national dish and, even if nowadays other countries copy it, it still remains the Italians' symbol throughout the world.

Today, women have gradually devoted less and less time to the kitchen board, the rolling pin, and the flour; being too busy at the office or socially. Thus it was necessary to invent something! Pasta machines were produced almost everywhere, but limited in their function: one needed to prepare the dough with flour and eggs separately, and to reach the proper consistency in order to turn the dough into a thin layer of pasta with the crank type machine. Too many phases to go through, before coming to the end result which was always the same: tagliatelle only. That is why it was necessary to do something; so the PastaMatic was made. The idea to build this extraordinary machine to make any possible kind of fresh pasta came in Italy, in Gessate, near Milan, in a factory, SIMAC, whose trademark has become synonymous for new alternatives in the ordinary production of small household appliances in the last decade.

SIMAC has done what was actually needed; a different kind of pasta machine, which is the phenomenon of our century! The PastaMatic has been created originally with a perfect structure, which still doesn't need to be changed or adjusted. SIMAC has turned the idea of functional capacity matched with a limited cost into a reality. The PastaMatic is successful because it made possible the preparation

of the same pasta Artusi wrote about, quickly at home, at a very low cost; without mess of any difficulty. Furthermore, it allows you to prepare not only tagliatelle, pappardelle and taglierini, but also the whole range of "dry" pastas: from common spaghetti to penne and conchiglie, plain or fluted bucatini and many more, (as only large pasta manufacturers can do). The PastaMatic offers 24 different extruding discs (and it still wants to go further). This incredible machine kneads the dough for pizza, pastries, bread, bread sticks, cookies, crackers and can be used for a hundred different purposes.

SIMAC's ideas are extremely diversified; its range of products is not limited to the PastaMatic but it also includes: "Il Gelataio" - The Ice Cream Man - to prepare soft and ordinary ice creams at home; the BravoSimac, a kitchen robot, which grinds, kneads, whips, juice extracts, juices and blends. The CaffèSimac for an Italian expresso coffee without going to Italy. The CombiVapor, a whole set of pots and pans, which can all be turned into a pressure cooker in a matter of seconds, with an exclusively designed CombiVapor lid and standard cookware lid.

This is how an innovative company operating in the sector of small household appliances becomes successful. SIMAC conceives, designs and manufactures a whole series of machines, meant to serve different specific functions with no confusion or overlapping of purpose, instead of conceiving and producing a "multipurpose" machine with the risk of performing poorly in almost everything.

Let's take "Il Gelataio" for example. There are two versions: The Ice Cream Man produces 1.2 quarts, and the Ice Cream Boy produces .6 quarts in one cycle. What a wonderful machine! It's fully automatic. Just add the ingredients as instructed by the recipe, push two buttons and "Il Gelataio" makes a perfectly genuine ice cream in 20 minutes ...and it doesn't need refrigeration because it is a completely self-contained refrigeration unit! The Ice Cream Man and Boy allow you to control the consistency you desire. Another example of how good SIMAC's ideas are, is the CombiVapor. Pressure cookers and stainless steel cookware can currently be found in many households, where at one time only a few households could afford them. Yet, they are still considered a separate pot from other ordinary kitchen tools on one side a pressure

cooker and on the other, ordinary cookware. The pressure cooker is meant and actually used for one single function, while the ordinary pots and pans serve different functions. SIMAC has conceived, designed and manufactured the CombiVapor. It is an entirely new system, which, thanks to a revolutionary lid, turns any standard pot into a pressure cooker in the time it takes to fit the lid into place! All CombiVapor pots and pans are provided with a special heat preserving Multitherm bottom.

In designing its whole range of products, SIMAC has always aimed at providing its customers with simple machines, which could be used easily and could also bring something new into the kitchen. SIMAC has actually introduced some novelties not only in the Italian kitchens, but also in other European countries and continents. Let's take Japan, the phenomenon of the 80's. Despite their well-established reputation as exporters, Japanese import from Italy SIMAC's products and in particular, "Il Gelataio" - The Ice Cream Man - which has received a terrific response.

In North America (namely in the U.S.A.) 25 people out of 100 who purchase the PastaMatic are of Italian origin, 75 are Anglo-Saxon, Slav, Spanish, or Scandinavian. Many have come to eat and appreciate Italian fresh pasta thanks to the PastaMatic.

It took several years of study to manufacture the PastaMatic and it is covered by such a great number of patents that it can be truly considered as the "quintessence" of technology. The PastaMatic was awarded in 1979 the Golden Medal at the "Salon de l'Alimentation et des Arts Ménagers" in Brussels.

If you examine the PastaMatic closely, or use it for just 5 minutes, you will realize how simple, tough, practical and almost "human" it is. In fact, the PastaMatic reproduces the action of man's hands kneading dough, essentially and perfectly. This is why the PastaMatic is so unique!

According to old rules and traditions, the mixture of flour and eggs or flour and water for fresh pasta, must be made with ever-increasing energy in order to make it even, consistent and flexible. The dough is to be rolled on the kitchen board first and then, when the dough processing is at its peak, it is to be pressed with a sliding movement of the palm energetically and vigorously. This was the only way to make fresh pasta with good re-

sults. Now, the PastaMatic does it the same way! The PastaMatic is provided with a special blade which simulates the movement of the hand mechanically (to realize how unique this blade is, suffice it to say that not even industrial pasta machines have something similar).

Once the dough has been kneaded, the blade pushes it towards the extruding screw, which in turn, forces the dough through the disc, turning it into tasty, consistently fresh pasta.

The PastaMatic is available in four versions: 700, 1000, 1400 and 3000 - specially created for restaurants and large communities. All four versions have something in common: they are practical and easy to use. You only need to add the ingredients and turn on the PastaMatic; in a few minutes pasta is ready to be cooked. Here is another speciality of the PastaMatic. You can make fresh pasta at the very last minute, while you are bringing the water to a boil, whereas once you would have needed to prepare it in the morning to serve it for lunch.

When kneading, the PastaMatic doesn't require any special care; you only have to check when the dough is ready to be extruded (when it is even, and smooth, presenting no trace of flour - the dough needs to be consistent and mustn't be sticky). At this point, you need only to choose one of the 24 discs, and the pasta is ready! After having used the PastaMatic a couple of times, you will come to know how and when to intervene and to compensate too wet a dough or excess moisture due to juices from some vegetables (it is possible to make green, red, brown pastas by adding parsley, basil, garlic and many possible herbs and vegetables) and always get perfect, tasty pasta. If you don't use up all of the dough you have prepared, do not discard, keep it in the refrigerator. The dough will remain fresh and tasty for a couple of weeks.

The PastaMatic is so easy to use, you can make perfect pasta to your choice, color and size, at the moment you like, and it is fun to make! This is why it has gained the favor of 46 countries. In the U.S., the PastaMatic is marketed coast-to-coast. It is also exported and very successful in Africa and in the Far East.

The PastaMatic is changing the eating habits of people all over the world. This is another success of the Italians' creativity and ability, and thanks to SIMAC, it shows that good ideas always work everywhere.

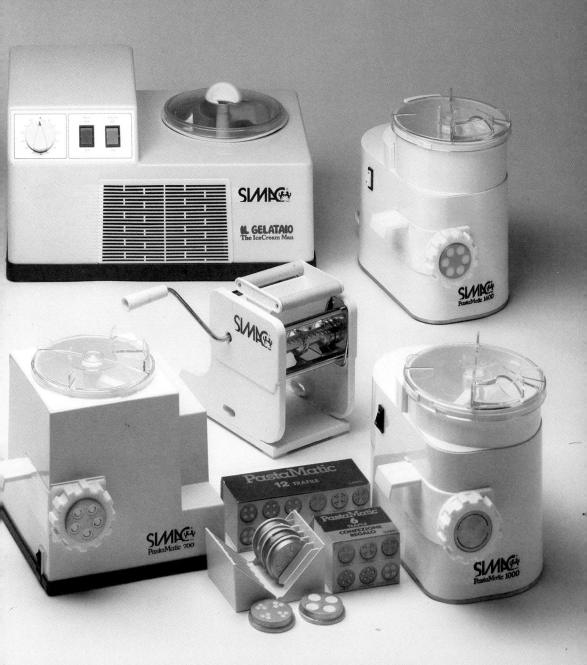

Assembly

1 - All removable parts are dishwasher safe and easily assembled in a matter of seconds.

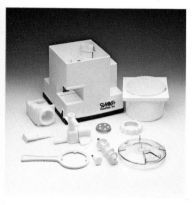

2 - Slide the rotary housing all the way into the open side of the base, ridged side down and rectangular opening facing up.

3 - Insert the bowl onto the base, matching the opening on the side of the bowl with the opening in the base and pressing down firmly.

4 - Fit the blade, kneading foot down over the central metal shaft extending up through the bowl.

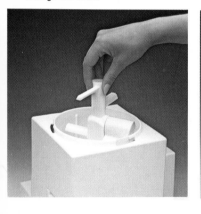

5 - Place the locking nut on top of the blade shaft and turn clockwise until it is firmly in place.

6 - Insert the rotary screw, metal end first, all the way into the rotary housing.

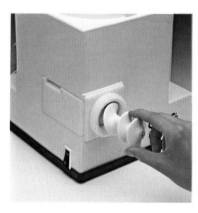

7 - Grasp the shutter slide, thumb grip up, and firmly push it all the way into the slot over the rotary housing.

8 - Flip the switch on the base to "on".

9 - Place the cover of the bowl and turn it counterclockwise to lock it into place.

General Procedure

MEASURING THE FLOUR

When measuring flour, always use the special PastaMatic cup. (fig. 1). Place the cup, with its grid top in place, on a flat surface. Spoon flour into the top and push it down through the holes. Do not shake or bang the flour into the cup or it will pack down and not give an even measure. Once the cup is full, swing the top away, leaving you with a level cup of flour which weighs approximately a half pound. For the purposes of this book, when we call for 1 pound flour, we mean flour measured twice as described.

MEASURING THE LIQUID

The PastaMatic has its own special liquid measuring cup. (fig. 2).
Examine it carefully. There are several liquid levels marked on the cup. On the left are indicated levels for water for 1/2 lb. flour and for 1 lb. flour. On the right are the levels for eggs. Notice that the egg levels are relatively higher than the water levels since eggs are denser than water. Also note that these levels cannot always be a precise guide because of the variability of the flour.

MAKING THE PASTA

When ready to make pasta, choose your recipe. (We recommend starting with a basic egg or water pasta as an introduction). Assemble the machine and plug it in. Do not put the cover on. Be sure the shutter slide is firmly in place. Have a clean surface or a plate ready to put the pasta on as it comes out of the machine. If using a metal disc, dip it in warm water before using. The pasta will be somewhat smoother. Measure the flour and dump the contents of each cup into the bowl. (fig. 3).

Measure the liquid according to the recipe. Place the cover on the bowl and turn it counterclockwise to lock it into place.
Turn the switch to "on", thereby starting the action of the blades. Begin very slowly to add the liquid to the flour, pouring it in tablespoon by tablespoon and letting the flour absorb the liquid before adding more. It should take a full minute to add all the liquid to the flour. (fig. 4).

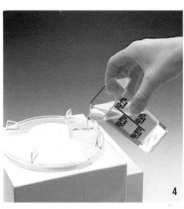

Let the machine run for another full minute (time it) to mix the flour. Then, turn the cover to stop the machine. Remove the lid.

Feel the dough with your fingers. It can be either too dry, too wet or just right. It is better if the dough is slightly drier than wetter.

Either way, it is important to correct the wetness at this early stage since it is difficult to do once the dough is well kneaded.

The dough is the proper consistency when it looks like moist, walnut-size lumps but not sticky. (fig. 5).

If the dough is too dry, it will feel floury. To correct, turn the machine on and slowly pour in another tablespoon water. Let run another minute and check again. If necessary, repeat.
If the dough is too wet, it will feel sticky. In that case, sprinkle 1 tablespoon flour evenly over the dough in the bowl. Replace the cover and run the machine for another minute. Check again and repeat, if necessary. Once the dough is of the proper consistency, let the machine run for the recommended kneading time remaining for the recipe. The total kneading times are indicated at the end of each recipe and that is the important timing to follow. For example, if the recipe requires kneading for a total of 5 minutes and it takes 3 minutes to get the dough to the correct consistency, knead the dough for 2 more minutes at the end to make a total of 5 minutes.

The more you work with the machine, the sooner you will know for sure when the dough reaches the correct consistency and when it is sufficiently kneaded.

Doughs for this machine should only be kneaded until they are in walnut-size pieces.

Do not let the dough knead enough to form a smooth ball. (Note that the preceding directions do not apply to cookie or gnocchi dough, which differs markedly from pastas. See specific recipe).
Once the dough is ready, remove the shutter slide. (fig. 6).

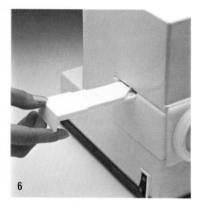
6

(If you wish to have greater control over the speed with which the pasta comes out of the machine, remove the shutter slide only partway). In less than a minute, the dough should begin coming through the opening. Stop the machine. Cut off the dough and push it through the hole in the cover to be mixed again with the rest of the dough. Select one of the pasta discs suggested in the recipe, and place it over the mouth of the housing, matching the teeth on the disc with the notches on the housing. (fig. 7).

7

Holding the disc in place with one finger in the center, fit the ring nut onto the rotary housing threads. (fig. 8).

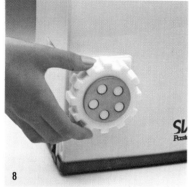
8

Using the wrench, turn it clockwise to tighten firmly. (fig. 9).

9

If the pasta is thin, the strands may stick together. To eliminate this problem, lightly oil or flour your hands and run your fingers through the pasta to coat it as it comes out of the machine. This step is not necessary for thicker doughs.
As the dough comes out of the machine, be ready to cut it either- with a knife or with floured scissors. Although it is not essential, try to make all the pieces the same size, especially for the smaller pastas. Evenly-cut sizes will all cook in the same amount of time.

(If you wish to make different shapes of pasta from the same batch, just stop the machine and remove the ring nut and disc. Set a new disc in place and replace the ring nut. Proceed with the extrusion).
Once most of the dough has been extruded, you may find that the blade does not push the dough through the opening in the bowl. If this happens, stop the machine and remove the cover. Break the remaining dough into pieces and push them down the hole. Replace the cover and turn the machine on again. The dough should now come through the disc.

NOTE: If the shutter slide is not fully in place and flour falls into the rotary housing, stop the machine at once and clean out the housing.
Flour must not clog the mechanism or it may seriously damage the machine.

WATER PASTA

1 pound all-purpose flour, measured in the PastaMatic cup; water to the water level for 1 pound flour.

Place the flour in the bowl and lock the cover in place. With the machine running, slowly pour in the water, as explained in the General Procedure. Add more water or flour as needed, letting the machine run for a minute after each addition. When the dough is of the correct consistency, let the machine run until the dough is properly kneaded.

Total mixing time will be 5 to 6 minutes.

Makes 1 1/3 pounds.

Recommended discs: All for pasta.

Cooking times: The round and flat pastas will cook in 1 to 3 minutes; the tubular pastas in 2-inch pieces will cook in 2 to 5 minutes.

Note: You can substitute quick-mixing flour for the all-purpose flour. Mix for about 7 minutes. Either way, for extra flavor you can add 2 tablespoons of olive oil to the dough after adding the water. Knead the dough an extra minute or two.

EGG PASTA

1 pound all-purpose flour, measured in the PastaMatic cup; eggs to the egg level for 1 pound flour (about 4 1/2 large eggs*).

Place the flour in the bowl and lock the cover in place. With the machine running, slowly pour in the eggs, as explained in the General Procedure. Add more egg or flour as needed, letting the machine run for a minute after each addition. When the dough is of the correct consistency, let the machine run until the dough is properly kneaded.

Total mixing time will be 6 to 7 minutes.

Makes 1 1/3 pounds.

Cooking times: The pastas will cook in 1 1/2 to 4 minutes.

* To use a partial egg, lightly scramble it before pouring it into the measure. You may substitute water for the partial egg.

WHOLE WHEAT PASTA

1/2 pound whole wheat flour, measured in the PastaMatic cup; 1/2 pound all-purpose flour, measured in the PastaMatic cup; water to the water level for 1 pound flour plus 1 tablespoon water. Place the flours in the bowl and lock the cover in place. With the machine running, slowly pour in the water, as explained in the General Procedure. Add more water or all-purpose flour as needed, letting the machine run for a minute after each addition. When the dough is of the correct consistency, let the machine run until the dough is properly kneaded. Total mixing time will be about 12 minutes.

Makes 1 1/3 pounds.

Cooking times: The pastas will cook in 2 to 4 minutes.

Note: If you like, add 2 tablespoons olive oil after the water. Knead an extra minute or two.

DURUM WHEAT OR SEMOLINA PASTA

By law, all pastas made in Italy are made from durum wheat, often from the grind called semolina. American boxed pastas may or may not be durum wheat; but they usually contain more water and therefore are softer upon cooking. Our semolina dough is very close - though fresher and thus better - to Italian pasta. Durum wheat - (semolina) flour - see directions in recipe; all-purpose flour - see directions in recipe; water to the water level for 1 pound flour. Fill the PastaMatic measuring cup with semolina flour. Put the flour in the bowl. Fill the cup again about halfway up with the semolina. Add all-purpose flour until the cup is full. Put the flours in the bowl and lock the cover in place. With the machine running, slowly pour in the water, as explained in the General Procedure. Add more water or all-purpose flour as needed, letting the machine run for a minute after each addition. When the dough is of the correct consistency, let the machine run until the dough is properly kneaded.

Total mixing time will be 7 to 8 minutes.

Makes about 1 1/3 pounds.

Cooking times. The round pastas will cook in 1 to 3 minutes; the tubular pastas in 2-inch pieces will cook in 2 to 4 minutes.

BUTTER COOKIES

5 ounces softened unsalted butter, 1 cup sugar; 1¹/₂ cups all-purpose flour; 1 large egg; 1 teaspoon vanilla extract.

Heat the oven to 350 °F.

Cut the butter into 8 pieces and put in the bowl with ¹/₄ cup sugar. Lock the cover in place and run the machine for a minute. With the machine still running, add another ¹/₄ cup sugar; knead a minute longer.

Add the remaining ¹/₂ cup sugar and knead 2 more minutes.

Stop the machine, add the flour, lock the cover in place and mix just until the flour is incorporated. With the machine running, add egg and vanilla and mix just until blended.

Have ready 2 or 3 ungreased baking sheets. Fit the machine with the cookie disc.

To extrude even cookies, pull out the shutter slide and let 2 inches of dough come out of the machine.

Stop the machine, cut off the dough, top cookie first, and place the strips on the cookie sheet, leaving an inch between cookies. (If you keep one hand under the top disc opening, you can catch the dough as it comes out and keep the cookies from sticking to each other). Repeat until all the dough is used.

Bake in the preheated oven for 10 minutes, or until lightly brown. Remove immediately to a rack to cool.

Makes 50 2-inch cookies.

Variations:

Lemon Cookies: Add the finely grated zest of 1 lemon to the dough with the vanilla.

Chocolate Cookies: Replace ¹/₂ cup flour with ¹/₂ cup unsweetened cocoa.

FRIED COOKIES

1 pound all-purpose flour, measured in the PastaMatic cup; $\frac{1}{3}$ cup sugar; 2 tablespoons vegetable oil; 4 large eggs; 2 egg yolks; 2 teaspoons vanilla extract.

For cooking: Vegetable oil; confectioner's sugar.

Place the flour and sugar in the bowl and lock the cover in place.

Run the machine for 30 seconds to mix. With the machine running, take 30 seconds to dribble in the oil. Slowly pour in the eggs, taking a full minute, then the egg yolks for another 30 seconds. Dribble in the vanilla extract. Add water or flour as needed, letting the machine run for a minute after each addition.

The dough should have the same consistency as pasta.

When it is of the correct consistency, let the machine run until the dough is properly kneaded.

Total mixing time will be about 5 minutes.

Cooking: Fit the machine with the lasagne disc, and extrude the dough in 4-inch pieces. In a wok or a saucepan, heat approximately 4 inches of vegetable oil to 375 °F.

Pinch each piece of dough in the center to make a bow-tie shape and cook them, 4 to 5 at a time, until golden brown, about a minute. Drain on a rack lined with wax paper and sprinkle with confectioners' sugar.

Makes 6 dozen 4-inch cookies.

POTATO GNOCCHI

1 pound Maine potatoes; $\frac{3}{4}$ cup all-purpose flour.

Scrub the potatoes under running water with a vegetable brush. Boil the unpeeled potatoes in a generous amount of water, covered with the lid ajar, for 50 to 55 minutes, or until done.

When cooked, drain thoroughly and peel. When cool enough to handle, quarter the potatoes and allow them to come to room temperature. This is very important so that the potatoes don't give off any heat or moisture in the machine. Put the potatoes through a ricer or food mill.

First put the flour into the bowl and then add the riced potatoes. Lock the cover in place. Let the machine run for 1 minute. The mixture will not be thoroughly blended.

Dust your fingers with flour, as the dough may be slightly sticky. Fit the machine with the gnocchi disc, and extrude the dough in 1" pieces, cutting them with a floured knife. Place the gnocchi on a lightly-floured board, then gently turn in the edges to form each gnocchi into a shell shape, ridged side out. Fill a wide skillet with about 2" of salted water and bring it to a boil. Lower the heat so the water simmers and add the gnocchi in a single layer. They should quickly float to the surface. Let them cook 10 seconds longer. Remove with a slotted spoon and keep warm. Continue in this way until all the gnocchi are cooked. Keep warm.

PIZZA WITH TOMATO AND CHEESE

Dough: 1 package (¹/₄-ounce) dry active yeast; 1 tablespoon sugar; warm water to the water level for 1 pound flour, less 2 tablespoons; 1 pound all-purpose flour, measured in the PastaMatic cup; 1 teaspoon salt; 2 tablespoons olive oil.

Add the yeast and sugar to the water. Set aside for 10 minutes.

Place the flour and salt in the bowl and lock the cover in place. Run the machine for 30 seconds to aerate the flour. With the machine running, take 30 seconds to dribble in the oil. Slowly pour in the dissolved yeast mixture, as explained in the General Procedure, letting the machine run for an extra minute.

Add more water or flour as needed, letting the machine run for a minute after each addition. The dough should have the same consistency as pasta. When it is of the correct consistency, let the machine run until the dough is properly kneaded.

Total mixing time will be about 8 minutes. Leave the dough in the machine with the cover in place to rise for 1¹/₂ hours, or until the dough doesn't bounce back when pressed with two fingers. Remove the dough from the bowl and briefly squeeze out the air. Tear the dough into walnut-size pieces and return them to the bowl.

Fit the machine with the pizza disc. Extrude the dough in one long piece. Cut it crosswise into three equal pieces. Place the three pieces barely overlapping on an oiled baking sheet. Wet the overlapping edges and work the pieces together with your fingers. You should have an approximate square. Turn about ¹/₂ inch dough under all around, then pinch the edges all around so you have a raised border. Brush the surface with olive oil. Cover with a kitchen towel and let rise for about 1 hour.

Assembly: 1 cup tomato sauce; 3 ounces thinly sliced mozzarella cheese.

Heat the oven to 400 °F.

Spread the tomato sauce on the dough and cover with the cheese.

Bake in the preheated oven for 20 to 30 minutes, or until the crust is brown.

Serves 4.

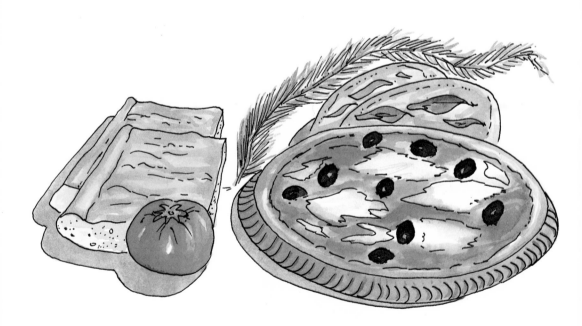

BREAD

1 pound of all-purpose flour; lukewarm water according to the water level for 1 lb. of flour, on the liquid measure cup; 1 teaspoon salt; $1/4$ oz. active dry yeast, 1 table-spoon sugar.

Follow the same steps as pizza dough. Pour the flour into the mixing bowl, dissolve the yeast in the lukewarm water. Slowly pour the water into the mixing bowl through the liquid intake hole.

Let the machine work for 8-10 minutes. Then stop the machine, let the mix rest for 10 minutes.

Unscrew the mixing blade screw. Pull out the mixing blade.

Pull the dough out of the mixing bowl, and shape into bread.

Leavening and baking bread

After having shaped the bread rolls, lay them on a baking sheet, sprinkled with flour, and keep them separated to prevent them from sticking, while rising. Cover them with cellophane or a kitchen cloth and allow to rise in a warm place, for instance near a radiator, or preheated oven. Leave the rolls covered in one place for at least 40 minutes to insure proper rising. When the size of the rolls has doubled, bake in the preheated oven (400-425 °F) for 20 to 30 minutes depending on the size of the rolls. The rolls will rise again during baking. It is suggested to place a metal bowl, containing hot water in the oven along with the bread. By evaporating, the water will keep the necessary moisture inside the oven. Do not open the oven for any reason whatsoever during the baking, otherwise temperature would drop, stopping the leavening process.

1 - CAPELLINI
(Angel's Hair)

2 - SPAGHETTI

3 - SPAGHETTONI
(Large Spaghetti)

4 - CHITARRE
(Square Spaghetti)

5 - LINGUINE

6 - TAGLIATELLE MEDIE
(Small Fettuccine)

7 - TAGLIATELLE
(Fettuccine)

8 - PAPPARDELLE
(Wide Fettuccine)

9 - SFOGLIE
(Lasagne)

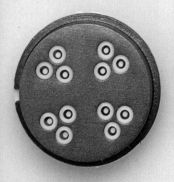

10 - BUCATINI
(Hollow Spaghetti)

11 - BUCATI RIGATI
(Hollow ridged Spaghetti)

12 - BUCATI
(Large hollow Spaghetti)

13 - PENNE
(Ziti)

14 - MACCHERONI
(Rigatoni)

15 - PIZZA

16 - BISCOTTI
(Cookies)

17 - GRISSINI
(Bread Sticks)

18 - GNOCCHI

19 - CONCHIGLIETTE RIGATE
(Small Shells)

20 - PASTA DEL CONTADINO
(Farmer's Pasta)

21 - FILI D'ORO
(Golden Threads)

22 - MACCHERONI QUADRA-
TI (Square Maccheroni)

23 - MACCHERONI QUADRI-
FOGLIO (Clover Leaf Mac-
cheroni)

24 - SFOGLIA REGOLABILE
PER RAVIOLI (Adjustable
wide width for ravioli)

Discs

Discs are one of the elements of the PastaMatic uniqueness. The PastaMatic, which is sold with 8 discs, kneads and produces an incredible number of different kinds of pasta, thanks to its range of 24 discs (for the moment being, they are just 24!) which have made it famous worldwide.

SIMAC steadily devotes its attention to the discs, so that it periodically invents some new ones.

Everybody knows that pasta changes in taste according to its shape: here is, therefore, the most reliable way to fight against dullness in the kitchen, the first enemy of appetite and good mood, when eating.

Discs can be purchased individually in department and gourmet specialty stores. Special disc holders with six discs are available. It is important noting that the latest discs have been manufactured according to a new concept, which allows an easier cleaning and a better quality of pasta: as a matter of fact, the new discs are made up by two parts; the inner part is made of brass and the outer one of Hostaform® a high quality, entirely nontoxic material which has been developed in the U.S. The two parts can be easily separated and they can be matched together in the same way. The cleaning is extremely easy. If you leave the parts until the dough dries, it is easiest to loosen the dough from the disc holes. Rap the disc sharply against the counter and the excess dough will fall right out. All discs are dishwasher safe.

Thanks to the PastaMatic, it will seem to you, as if you had a pasta factory at your house. But what pasta factory can provide you with such a great variety of shapes - and flavors - by merely changing a disc, or by varying the basic ingredients (durum, whole, all-purpose or buck wheat flour) or by adding vegetables or other ingredients, which can give the dough a particular taste?

Because of the big variety of pasta, tastes and ingredients, we thought it both useful and necessary to provide each recipe with all the information which will allow you to assess the cooking time, the skill needed and the most suitable wine for each dish by merely looking at the symbols (clock, cook's hat and bottle).

LEGEND

cooking time (time needed to prepare the dish from the beginning to when it should be served)

easy

fairly difficult

difficult

recommended wine

This will allow you to choose each recipe according to the time available to prepare it and - why not - according to the mood you are in. You either cannot always or are not always willing to spend two hours to prepare a first course dish when you can choose among many others equally tasty and delicious, which take 15 minutes only.

The PastaMatic enables you to cope practically with the daily problem of choosing what to serve for lunch or dinner in order to make each meal a joyful feast rather than a boring repetition. Common sense helps a lot, doesn't it?!

Furthermore, your imagination can run wild and match the strangest and most uncommon ingredients together: for example, what about pasta with pumpkin, with nettles, with cocoa powder, or hot pasta with anchovy or even pasta with cheese, which is so mild and nutritious?

Do you love gastronomic traditions? The PastaMatic will allow you to prepare any Italian regional speciality, from "pisarei" to "pizzoccheri", from "Genoa Easter pie" to Naples "Pastiera", in the shortest possible span of time, easily and also enjoying yourselves.

Are you a gourmand? With the help of this extraordinary machine you will be able to prepare a limitless variety of both sweet and salted cookies, easy-to-make and tasty cakes. Everything will be genuine and simple and you will choose the ingredients. Your cakes will contain no food dyes, no additives and no chemicals to preserve them at all and therefore you will give them even to your kids with no hesitation.

The PastaMatic is a machine to be used: do not put it away and do not remember to use it only once in a while, but keep it handy: it will be ready to serve you and it will easily turn your gastronomic ideas into a reality.

A SPECIAL NOTE

Each recipe calls for the purest quality ingredients. We highly recommend using the specific ingredients, to insure the best results (for example: fresh vegetables, pure imported extra-virgin olive oil, imported Italian Parmesan cheese Parmigiano Reggiano, imported Italian peeled tomatoes, fresh boletus mushrooms, etc.).
Buon Appetito!

Capellini

Also called Vermicellini or better known in America as Capelli d'Angelo (Angel's Hair).
Recommended kind of dough: With eggs
Cooking time: 2 minutes
To be used: For soups (2 ounces per portion) - drained (4 ounces per portion)
Variations: Capocchie di Spillo. Cut the pasta lengthwise into ¼" long pieces. To be used with meat or chicken broth. **Fidelini:** To be used with meat or vegetable broth. Cut the pasta lengthwise into 2-3" long-pieces.

Capellini with anchovy sauce

 About 18 minutes

Calories per portion: 540

Martina Franca bianco (Apulia) (white)

For four: *1 pound capellini - 6 flat anchovy fillets - 4 tablespoons butter - 1 cup of cream - salt and pepper.*

Instructions: Heat the anchovies and butter over low heat; mash the anchovies with a wooden spoon until they have turned into a paste. Pour in the cream and cook over low heat for 4-5 minutes. Cook the capellini in abundant, boiling, salted water. After 2 minutes drain and transfer into a preheated serving bowl. Pour the anchovy sauce over capellini and toss through. Serve immediately.

Capellini with gorgonzola cheese sauce

 About 15 minutes

Calories per portion: 764

Montelio bianco (Lombardy) (white)

For four: *1 pound capellini - 5 ounces mild gorgonzola cheese or Blue Cheese - 4 tablespoons butter - 1 cup of cream - 2-3 fresh sage leaves - salt and pepper - grated Parmesan cheese.*

Instructions: Melt the gorgonzola cheese with the butter and sage leaves in a small pan; add the cream, and pepper and stir constantly till smooth. Sprinkle the capellini with the grated Parmesan cheese and toss the cheese sauce through the capellini. Serve immediately.

Capellini with gorgonzola cheese sauce

Capellini with white sauce (au gratin)

 About 55 minutes

Calories per portion: 703

 Trebbiano di Aprilia (Latium) (white)

For four: 1 pound capellini - 4 level table-spoons potato flour - 3 cups milk - 6 table-spoons butter - salt and pepper - a pinch of grated nutmeg - 4 tablespoons Parmesan cheese - 2 eggs - 5 tablespoons cream - 3 tablespoons fine breadcrumbs.

Instructions: Mix the potato flour with the milk and stir constantly to keep a smooth texture. Simmer on low heat, stirring constantly to allow the mixture to thicken. When the sauce comes to a boil, add the butter, salt, pepper, nutmeg and half of the grated cheese. Turn the heat off and beat the ingredients with a fork to blend. Pour in the egg yolks and the whites should be whipped until thick - blend the yolks in the sauce separately.
Cook the capellini in abundant, boiling, salted water and drain after one minute of cooking time. Return the capellini to the same pan and add both the cream sauce and the eggwhite sauce with the grated cheese and toss through. Transfer to a heat-resistant glass pan, which has been greased with butter and the breadcrumbs. Add diced pieces of butter and cheese to the top and bake at 350 °F, until it turns golden brown color on top, 5-8 minutes.

Capocchie di spillo with spinach

 About 40 minutes

Calories per portion: 300

 Müller-Thurgau (Trentino-Alto Adige) (white)

For four: 1/2 pound capocchie di spillo - 1 cup fresh spinach - 1 leek - 4 tablespoons butter - 1 beef stock cube - 9 cups water - grated Parmesan cheese.

Instructions: Wash and slice the leek finely, discarding the very tips. Saute over low heat with the butter in a large soup pot. Pour in the water, stock cube, and salt and bring to a boil. Wash the fresh spinach thoroughly, drain, and cut the leaves into small strips. Add the spinach to the water and cook about 10 minutes. Drop the capocchie di spillo into the soup and cook for 5 minutes; serve with a topping of grated Parmesan cheese.

Capocchie di spillo with tomato puree

 About 1 hour

Calories per portion: 425

Tocai delle Grave del Friuli (Friuli) (white)

For four: *½ pound capocchie di spillo - 1 pound of fresh tomatoes - 1 medium size onion - 4-5 fresh basil leaves - ½ chicken stock cube - 2 tablespoons butter - ½ cup cream - 3 cups milk - 4 cups water - grated Parmesan cheese - salt and pepper.*

Instructions: Dice the tomatoes and cook with the chopped onion and the diced basil leaves for 10 minutes. Press through a food mill or blender to get a puree. In a large pan, add the puree, butter, cream, water, milk, and stock cube - and bring to a boil - then simmer for an additional 15 minutes. Stir in the capocchie di spillo and cook for 5 minutes. Add salt and pepper and stir; serve with the grated Parmesan cheese.

Fidelini soup

 About 35 minutes

Calories per portion: 222

Cortese dei Colli Tortonesi (Piedmont) (white)

For four: *½ pound fidelini - 8 ounces fresh peas (or use frozen peas) - ½ cup chopped Italian parsley - 9 cups beef broth - salt and pepper - 4 tablespoons grated Parmesan cheese.*

Instructions: Cook the peas in the broth for 20 minutes. Add the chopped parsley, salt and pepper and the fidelini and cook for 5 minutes. Serve with grated Parmesan cheese on top.

Spaghetti

Also called Bigoli or Vermicelli

Recommended kind of dough: With eggs - with durum wheat flour

Cooking time: 4 minutes - 3 minutes for firm texture -

To be used: For soups (2½ ounces per portion) - drained (4 ounces per portion)

Variations: Tempestina. To be used for soups with chicken or meat broths. Cut the pasta lengthwise into ¼" long pieces. **Small spaghetti.** To be used with vegetable or meat broths. Cut the pasta lengthwise into 3-4" long pieces.

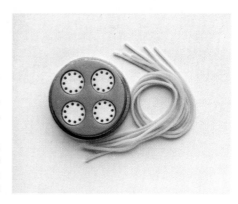

Spaghetti with clam sauce

 About 45 minutes

Calories per portion: 775

 Falerno bianco (Campania) (white)

For four: 1 pound spaghetti - 2 dozen small clams - 1 pound peeled fresh plum tomatoes (or 2 cups tomato sauce) - 2 garlic cloves - ¼ cup chopped parsley - 6 tablespoons olive oil - salt and pepper.

Instructions: Wash and scrub the clams thoroughly and transfer them into a large covered frying pan. Cook with enough water to cover the clams over a medium heat until they are open. Discard all the clams which do not open from their shells. Remove the clams from their shells and set aside. Saute the garlic in oil over low heat until it becomes golden brown and discard the excess. Add the tomatoes and cook over medium heat stirring in the clam juice for about 10 minutes. Slowly add the clams and the parsley - then simmer for 1-2 minutes. Cook the spaghetti in salted, boiling water and drain. Put the spaghetti back to the warm pan, and pepper, toss with the clam sauce.

Housewife's soup

 About 1 hour

Calories per portion: 377

 Merlot dei Colli Orientali Friulani (Friuli-Venezia Giulia) (red)

For four: ½ pound tempestina - 1 medium size onion - 1 potato - 1 carrot - 1 stalk celery - ½ pound fresh or frozen asparagus - 4 tablespoons butter - 1 teaspoon salt - 2 tablespoons cream - grated Parmesan cheese - a pinch of cinnamon powder - 10½ cups chicken or beef broth (or use stock cubes with water).

Instructions: Dice the onion, potato, carrot, celery and tip of the asparagus; saute in butter until tender and season with cinnamon and salt. Pour in the broth and bring to a boil, then allow to continue cooking over medium heat for 30 minutes or until the vegetables are cooked to your taste of firmness. About five minutes before the cooking time is completed add the tempestina and the asparagus to the soup; stir in the cream and serve with a topping of grated Parmesan cheese.

Spaghetti with sage

  About 15 minutes

Calories per portion: 515

Orvieto classico (Umbria) (white)

For four: *1 pound spaghetti - 4 tablespoons butter - 6 fresh sage leaves or 2 teaspoons dried sage leaves - grated Parmesan cheese - salt and pepper.*

Instructions: Heat the butter over low heat until it starts to foam; add the sage leaves and stir; cook for 5 minutes. Remove the sage leaves and add salt and pepper to taste.
Cook the spaghetti in abundant, salted, boiling water until firm to the bite; drain and sprinkle with Parmesan cheese. Pour the sauce over the spaghetti and toss through. Serve in heated bowls (placed in hot water then dried). Add more Parmesan cheese to the top.

Spaghetti with egg sauce

 About 15 minutes

Calories per portion: 518

Castel del Monte rosato (Apulia) (rosé)

For four: *1 pound spaghetti - 4 tablespoons grated Parmesan cheese - 1/4 cup diced parsley - 6 tablespoons butter - salt and pepper.*

Instructions: Cook the pasta in abundant, boiling, salted water while you prepare the sauce. Melt the butter in a small pan over low heat. Beat the eggs and add the salt and pepper and the parsley with the Parmesan cheese. Drain the spaghetti and transfer into a preheated serving bowl. Pour the sauce over the pasta and toss; allow to thicken (2 minutes). Add more cheese if desired.

Spaghetti with aubergines (eggplants) and pesto sauce

 About 40 minutes

Calories per portion: 655

 Coronata bianco (Liguria) (white)

For four: 1 pound spaghetti - 4 small eggplants - 1/2 cup pesto sauce (as instructed on page 82) - 4 tablespoons butter - grated Parmesan cheese.

Instructions: Wash and dice the eggplants without peeling them. Drop in abundant, salted water and allow to cook for 15 minutes.
Cook the pasta in the same boiling water; cook until firm to the bite.
Transfer the pasta and the eggplants into a preheated serving bowl and toss the butter and grated Parmesan cheese through the pasta. Add the pesto sauce and toss through; serve the pasta immediately.

Spaghetti with chicken livers

 About 20 minutes

Calories per portion: 565

 Traminer del Collio (Friuli-Venezia Giulia) (white)

For four: 1 pound spaghetti - 1 pound chicken livers - 4 tablespoons butter - 1 medium onion - 1/2 cup dry white wine - 2 bay leaves - 1/2 teaspoon dried marjoran - a pinch of cinnamon powder - salt and pepper.

Instructions: Chop the onion and saute in butter over low heat until it turns a golden brown color. Add the pre-chopped chicken livers, crushed bay leaves, and cinnamon and cook over medium heat for ten minutes.
Pour in the wine and add the marjoran and cook for 5-8 minutes; add salt and pepper to taste. After the pasta is cooked and drained, add the sauce and toss through. Serve immediately.

41

Porto spaghetti sauce

 About 40 minutes

Calories per portion: 726

Cinque Terre (Liguria) (white)

For four: *1 pound spaghetti - ¹/₂ pound ham - 1 carrot - 1 stalk of celery - 3 shallot onions - 4 tablespoons butter - ¹/₂ cup dry red wine - ¹/₂ cup coffee - 4 tablespoons grated Parmesan cheese - salt and pepper.*

Instructions: Dice the carrot, celery, and onions; saute in butter until tender. Mince the ham and cook with the vegetables for 15 minutes. Add the wine and coffee and cook for 8-10 minutes.
After the pasta has been cooked and drained, toss with the sauce and add Parmesan cheese to the top.

Spaghetti with chocolate sauce

 About 15 minutes

Calories per portion: 796

Alto Adige Riesling Italico (Alto Adige) (white)

For four: *1 pound spaghetti - 4 oz of bitter chocolate - 1 cup cream - ¹/₂ cup cognac or brandy - a pinch of grated nutmeg - 4 tablespoons grated Parmesan cheese - salt and pepper.*

Instructions: Chop the chocolate into small pieces; add the cream and cook over low heat until the chocolate is melted. Add the nutmeg and cognac and allow to simmer for 3-4 minutes. When the pasta is cooked and drained, toss with sauce and sprinkle the Parmesan cheese on top of each bowl.

Small spaghetti with vegetable "Julienne" soup

 About 1 hour

Calories per portion: 342

 Verdiso della Marca Trevigiana (Venetia) (white)

For four: *½ pound small spaghetti - 2 carrots - 2 stalks of celery - 1 medium onion - 1 zucchini - 4 ounces fresh peas - ½ cup diced fresh spinach - 4 plum tomatoes - 1 ounce butter - 2 tablespoons olive oil - 9 cups chicken broth - grated Parmesan cheese - salt and pepper.*

Instructions: Peel the tomatoes and chop all the vegetables (either with ordinary kitchen tools or with BravoSimac) and saute in the butter and oil, stirring constantly until all the vegetables have absorbed the cooking fats. Pour in the broth (preheated) and add the salt, pepper and cheese; bring to a boil and add the pasta; cook 4-5 minutes. Sprinkle with more cheese on top of each serving if desired.

Spaghetti with olive oil and garlic

 About 15 minutes

Calories per portion: 625

 Marino (Latium) (white)

For four: *1 pound spaghetti - 8 tablespoons olive oil - 1 tablespoon diced chili pepper - 3 cloves garlic - ¼ cup chopped parsley.*

Instructions: Heat the cloves of garlic and chili pepper in the olive oil, crushing the cloves of garlic with a fork for more taste. Then remove the excess garlic and chili pepper. Cook the pasta and drain it. Toss the spaghetti with the sauce and top with the chopped parsley.

Spaghetti with brandy sauce

 About 55 minutes

Calories per portion: 761

Colli Euganei rosso (Venetia) (red)

For four: 1 pound spaghetti - 1 clove garlic - 1 medium onion - 4 tablespoons butter - 4 tablespoons olive oil - 1 cup tomato puree - 1/2 cup brandy - 3 cups cream - pinch of grated nutmeg - salt and pepper.

Instructions: Chop the garlic and onion very fine, and saute in butter and oil over low heat for a few minutes; add the tomato puree and allow to cook for about 30 minutes. Pour in the brandy, salt and pepper and cook for 5 minutes. Cook the spaghetti and drain; season with nutmeg and toss with the cream. Add the sauce and toss thoroughly. Serve immediately.

Spaghetti "alla puttanesca"

 About 30 minutes

Calories per portion: 571

Vesuvio (Campania) (red)

For four: 1 pound spaghetti - 1 pound fresh peeled plum tomatoes or 2 cups tomato sauce - 12 black olives - 4 tablespoons butter - 3 tablespoons olive oil - 4 flat anchovy fillets - 1 tablespoon capers - 1 tablespoon chopped parsley - 5 basil leaves - 2 cloves of garlic - salt and pepper - dash of crushed red pepper.

Instructions: Saute the cloves of garlic in the oil and the butter until it becomes golden brown in color, then discard. Add the diced tomatoes, capers, chopped and pitted olives and minced anchovy fillets; allow to cook over medium heat for about 10 minutes, then add the parsley and diced basil leaves. Taste for desired salt and pepper. Cook and drain the pasta, then toss with the sauce and serve immediately in heated bowls.

Spaghetti with cuttle-fish and black liquid sauce

 About 45 minutes

Calories per portion: 605

 Collio Pinot bianco (Friuli-Venezia Giulia) (white)

For four: *1 pound spaghetti - 1 medium size onion - ½ pound cuttle-fish tentacles - 2 cuttle-fish with black liquid sacs - 1 pound peeled tomatoes - 6 tablespoons olive oil - salt and pepper - (Calamari can be used in place of the cuttle-fish).*

Instructions: Chop the onion and saute it in the olive oil until golden brown in color. Add the tomatoes (finely chopped) and the minced cuttle-fish tentacles (or Calamari tentacles), and cook over low heat for 10 minutes. Add salt, pepper and the cuttle-fish (or diced Calamari) black liquid and continue cooking for 10 more minutes. Cook and drain the spaghetti, toss with the sauce and serve immediately.

Tempestina with artichoke soup

 About 1 hour

Calories per portion: 366

Alto Adige Riesling Italico (Trentino-Alto Adige) (white)

For four: *½ pound tempestina (dough with eggs) - 3 medium size fresh artichokes - ½ pound fresh peas - 1 chicken stock cube - 4 tablespoons butter - 2 ounces Swiss Emmenthal Cheese (use aged Swiss Cheese if you cannot find this brand) - 1 cup milk - 3 cups water - salt and pepper.*

Instructions: Prepare the artichokes - remove the leaves and keep the tender hearts only - boil them with the peas in enough water to cover them. Press the vegetables through a food mill or sieve and add the artichoke and pea puree to their cooking water. Stir in the milk and water and bring to a boil; drop in the stock cube, salt, pepper and butter. After 8-10 minutes, drop in the pasta and the coarsely grated Swiss Cheese, stirring constantly to allow the cheese to melt evenly. Taste for additional salt and pepper; serve immediately.

Spaghettoni

Recommended kind of dough: With wholewheat - with durum wheat flour
Cooking time: 8 minutes - 10 minutes
To be used: Drained (4 ounces per portion)

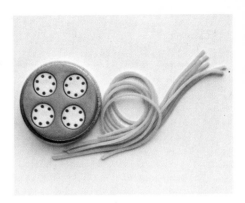

15th of August spaghettoni

 About 1 hour and 15 minutes

Calories per portion: 708

 Bianchello del Metauro (Marche) (white)

For four: 1 pound spaghettoni - 1 pound plum tomatoes - 3 ¹/₂ ounces tuna fish (canned-without oil) - 1 small eggplant - 1 tablespoon capers - 10 green olives - 7-8 fresh basil leaves - 1 clove of garlic - 3 shallot onions - 1 carrot - 1 stalk celery - 8 tablespoons olive oil - salt and pepper.

Instructions: Wash and chop the tomatoes, eggplant, olives, garlic, onions, carrot, celery and the basil leaves. Cook the tomatoes with 3 tablespoons of oil, the basil, garlic, onion, carrot, celery, and salt - stirring often - for 10 minutes. Cover and allow to simmer for 40 minutes. Press the vegetable mixture through a food mill or sieve with the cooking juices; add the olive oil and mix throuth with some pepper and set aside.
Wash the eggplant and cook in olive oil for about 8 minutes. Cook and drain the pasta, then toss with the vegetable sauce, diced eggplant, crushed tuna fish, capers and green olives.

Spaghettoni with olives - Sicilian style

 About 40 minutes

Calories per portion: 640

 Regaleali bianco (Sicily) (white)

For four: 1 pound spaghettoni - 1 pound peeled plum tomatoes or 1 cup tomato sauce - 2 cloves of garlic - 6 tablespoons olive oil - 24 black olives - 2 tablespoons capers - 1 chili pepper - ¹/₂ cup milk - 1 tablespoon chopped Italian parsley - salt and pepper.

Instructions: Heat the garlic and chili pepper in the oil, then remove after 2-3 minutes. Remove the stones from the olives and chop with the tomatoes; then add the olives, tomatoes and capers to the oil and cook for 10 minutes. Pour in the milk and cook for another 10 minutes. Add salt and pepper and the chopped parsley.
Cook and drain the pasta and toss with the sauce.

15th of August Spaghettoni

Spaghettoni with olives-Sicilian style

Spaghettoni with herb and ricotta cheese sauce

 About 35 minutes

Calories per portion: 714

 Frascati (Latium) (white)

For four: *1 pound spaghettoni - 8 fresh basil leaves - 4 sage leaves or ¹/₂ teaspoon dried sage leaves - ¹/₂ teaspoon Italian herb seasoning - ¹/₄ cup chopped parsley - 2 tablespoons capers - 10 black olives - 6 tablespoons olive oil - 1 cup ricotta cheese - 1 cup cream - 4 tablespoons grated Romano cheese - salt and pepper.*

Instructions: Remove the stones from the olives and chop them along with the herbs. Saute the olives and herbs in the olive oil for 10 minutes. Add the ricotta cheese, the cream and the salt and allow to simmer for 5 minutes. Cook and drain the pasta, toss with the sauce and add the Romano cheese and pepper and mix through. Serve hot.

Three flavor spaghettoni

 About 55 minutes

Calories per portion: 740

 Rosa del Golfo (Apulia) (rosé)

For four: *1 pound spaghettoni - 4 tablespoons olive oil - 2 cloves of garlic - 4 flat anchovy fillets - 16 peeled tomatoes or 3 cups tomato sauce - ¹/₂ cup cooking juices from a roast - salt and pepper.*

Instructions: Crush the garlic and anchovies and cook over low heat for a few minutes; add the diced tomatoes or sauce, salt and pepper and cook for 10 minutes. Pour in the cooking juice and mix; cook for 25 minutes.
Cook and drain the pasta. Toss through with the sauce.

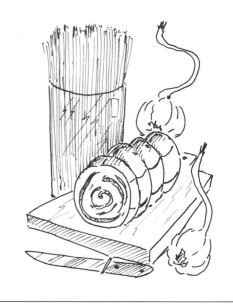

Spaghettoni with Argentinian sauce

  About 45 minutes

Calories per portion: 638

Valpolicella classico superiore (Venetia) aged 2 years (red)

For four: 1 pound spaghettoni - ¹/₂ pound of ground meat - 12 ounces tomato puree - 1 medium onion - 1 clove garlic - 6 table-spoons olive oil - dash of cinnamon pow-der - grated Parmesan cheese - salt and pepper.

Instructions: Chop the onion and garlic and heat in the oil with the cinnamon powder for a few minutes; add the ground meat, saute for 5 minutes, stir often. Add the tomato puree and cook over low heat for 20 minutes. Add salt and pepper, and pour over pasta that has been cooked and drained. Sprinkle Parmesan cheese on top of each serving.

Spaghettoni with soybean sprouts

  About 20 minutes

Calories per portion: 530

Parrina bianco (Tuscany) (white)

For four: 1 pound spaghettoni - 1 cup soybean sprouts - 2 cloves of garlic - 1 small chili pepper - 6 flat anchovy fillets - 1 tablespoon chopped parsley - 6 table-spoons olive oil - salt.

Instructions: Rinse the soybean sprouts and dry; cook a few minutes over a low heat with the olive oil, garlic, chopped chili pepper, mashed anchovies, stirring constantly, then add the salt and parsley. Cook and drain pasta, toss it with the sauce.

Chitarre *(Square spaghetti)*

Recommended kind of dough: With wholewheat flour-with durum wheat flour
Cooking time: 8 minutes-10 minutes
To be used: Drained (4 ounces per portion)

Chitarre with ragu meat sauce

 About 1 hour and 50 minutes

Calories per portion: 772

 Anagni rosso (Latium) (red)

For four: 1 pound chitarre - 4 tablespoons butter - 2 tablespoons olive oil - 2 slices pancetta or bacon - 1 small onion - 1 carrot - 1 stalk celery (with the leaves) - 1 clove garlic - 2 bay leaves - ¹/₂ pound ground beef - ¹/₂ cup red wine - 2 tablespoons tomato puree - grated Parmesan cheese - salt and pepper.

Instructions: Chop the pancetta or bacon and saute in butter and oil with the bay leaves. Chop the vegetables and saute for 10 minutes; then add the ground beef - stir constantly for 5-6 minutes. Pour in the wine and cook for 5 minutes. Dilute the tomato puree with 2 tablespoons of water and add to the sauce; simmer over low heat for one hour. Cook and drain the pasta; toss with the ragu sauce and sprinkle with the cheese.

Chitarre with beer sauce

 About 1 hour

Calories per portion: 596

 Light Beer - Peroni

For four: 1 pound chitarre - 4 tablespoons olive oil - 1 cup light beer - 1 clove of garlic - 1 sweet yellow pepper - 8 plum tomatoes - 8 green olives - 4 tablespoons chopped parsley - 1 teaspoon marjoran - 4 flat anchovies - 1 tablespoon capers - salt and pepper - grated Parmesan cheese.

Instructions: Wash and dice the pepper, tomatoes, olives, parsley, garlic, anchovies. Saute the ingredients in the oil and stir in the beer gradually after 8-10 minutes. Then add the anchovies, capers, parsley and marjoran; cook for 10 minutes and add the pepper.
Cook and drain the pasta; toss with the grated Parmesan cheese, then the sauce.

Chitarre with ragu meat sauce

Chitarre with beer sauce

Chitarre with onions, anchovies and oregano

About 45 minutes

Calories per portion: 541

Montepulciano d'Abruzzo (Abruzzo) (red)

For four: *1 pound chitarre - 1 large onion - 2 ounces flat anchovy fillets - 1/4 cup olive oil - 1 teaspoon Italian herb seasoning - 1/2 cup dry white wine - Parmesan cheese.*

Instructions: Saute the onion in part of the oil until translucent in color - add the anchovies, mashing with a wooden spoon. Add the Italian herb seasoning and the wine and cook over low heat for 5-8 minutes.
Cook and drain the pasta; toss with the remaining oil and Parmesan cheese - then toss through with the sauce. Sprinkle more cheese on top.

Chitarre with infernal sauce ("hot sauce")

About 30 minutes

Calories per portion: 562

Monte Procida rosso (Campania) aged 1 year (red)

For four: *1 pound chitarre - 1 pound peeled tomatoes - 2 cloves garlic - 1/4 cup olive oil - 1/2 cup black olives - 2 tablespoons capers - 1 chili pepper - 4 tablespoons parsley - 1 teaspoon Worcester sauce - salt.*

Instructions: Crush the garlic and saute with the chili pepper in oil until golden brown in color, then discard garlic and pepper. Add the chopped tomatoes and pitted and chopped olives with the capers, Worcester sauce and salt; cook over medium heat for 15 minutes. Remove from heat and add the chopped parsley.
Cook and drain the pasta, toss it with the sauce and Parmesan cheese and serve immediately.

Chitarre salad

 About 15 minutes

Calories per portion: 590

 Solopaca bianco (Campania) (white)

For four: 1 pound chitarre - 6 plum tomatoes - 6 tablespoons olive oil - 1 clove garlic - 1 tablespoon chopped parsley - salt and pepper.

Instructions: Peel and chop the tomatoes, toss with the olive oil and the crushed garlic; sprinkle with the parsley, salt and pepper.
Cook and drain the pasta and rinse in cold water (to stop the cooking process). Add the cold sauce and toss thoroughly. (Best if the pasta marinates in the sauce for at least 30 minutes).

Chitarre with double cream

  About 35 minutes

Calories per portion: 813

Rosso dell'Oltrepò Pavese (Lombardy) aged 1 year (red)

For four: 1 pound chitarre - 1 cup double cream - 1 egg yolk - 4 tablespoons brandy - 1 cup fresh or frozen peas - 2 tablespoons chopped parsley - 4 tablespoons butter - salt and pepper.

Instructions: Beat the egg yolk with the brandy for a few minutes; add the cream and whip the sauce until it gets smooth; add the salt and pepper.
Saute the peas in the butter for 5 minutes; add the chopped parsley.
Cook and drain the pasta; toss first with the cream sauce then the peas. Serve immediately.

Linguine

Also called Tagliolini or Trenette
Recommended kind of dough: With eggs
Cooking time: 3 minutes
To be used: Drained (4 ounces per portion)
Variation: Assi di quadri. To be used with both meat or vegetable broth. Cut the pasta lengthwise into 3-4" long pieces.

Linguine with pink sauce

 About 1 hour

Calories per portion: 695

 Colli Mantovani del Garda Chiaretto (Lombardy) (rosé)

For four: 1 pound linguine - 1 tablespoon plain flour - 3 ounces butter - 2 cups milk - 1 egg yolk - 1/4 pound ham - 1 cup tomato puree - 3 tablespoons grated Parmesan cheese - dash of nutmeg - salt and pepper.

Instructions: Melt 1 ounce of butter over low heat and stir in the flour and milk; remove from the heat and stir constantly to keep the sauce smooth and thick. Heat the sauce again (low heat) and add the 3 tablespoons of Parmesan cheese, salt pepper and nutmeg and stir; remove from heat and let the sauce cool. When the sauce is lukewarm, add the egg yolk and stir through. Saute the ham in the 1 ounce of butter with the tomato puree for 15 minutes. Add the ham and tomato puree to the milk sauce and stir well to blend through the ingredients.
Cook and drain the pasta; toss with Parmesan cheese, then the sauce. Serve immediately.

Linguine with San Remo sauce

 About 35 minutes

Calories per portion: 672

 Vermentino di Imperia (Liguria) (white)

For four: 1 pound linguine - 1/2 cup tomato puree - 4 tablespoons butter - 6 tablespoons pesto sauce (as instructed on page 82) - 1/2 cup cream - 8 green olives - 2 tablespoons pine nuts - 4 walnuts - grated Parmesan cheese - 1/4 pound ham - salt and pepper.

Instructions: Pit and chop the olives. Chop the ham and nuts and set aside.
Heat the butter with the tomato puree in a large saute pan and allow to cook for 10 minutes. Remove from heat and add the cream and the pesto sauce, stirring constantly to blend thoroughly.
Cook and drain the pasta; sprinkle with Parmesan cheese and toss.
Add the olives, ham and nuts and mix through the pasta; add the sauce to the pasta and blend through. Serve immediately.

Linguine with chicken ragu sauce

 About 1 hour and 20 minutes

Calories per portion: 583

Grignolino d'Asti (Piedmont) aged 1 year (red)

For four: *1 pound linguine - 1 medium onion - 1 pound chicken breasts - 2 tablespoons olive oil - 4 tablespoons butter - 2 bay leaves - 1/2 cup dry white wine - 1/2 cup fresh or canned tomato puree - 2 tablespoons milk - 1 tablespoon chopped parsley - grated Parmesan cheese - salt and pepper.*

Instructions: Chop and saute the onion in oil until it becomes golden brown in color; add the minced chicken breasts and the bay leaves; saute for 5-8 minutes (until white and not pink) and add the white wine and cook 5 minutes; add the tomato puree, milk and salt and pepper and cook about 35-40 minutes. Add the chopped parsley and taste for more salt or pepper. Cook and drain the pasta and toss thoroughly first with the cheese then with the ragu sauce. Serve immediately.

Linguine "mountain style"

 About 1 hour and 10 minutes

Calories per portion: 550

Carema (Piedmont) aged 1 year (red)

For four: *1 pound linguine - 4 tablespoons butter - 2 ounces dried mushrooms - 1 tablespoon potato flour - 1 tablespoon minced parsley - 3-4 sage leaves - 1 cup chicken broth - grated Parmesan cheese - salt and pepper.*

Instructions: Soak the mushrooms in lukewarm water for about 1/2 hour; wash and chop the mushrooms, then saute them in 2 tablespoons of butter over low heat for 15 minutes. Pour in chicken broth gradually; add the potato flour, sage leaves, remaining butter and parsley; stir and allow to thicken for 20-25 minutes. Add salt and pepper and stir.
Cook and drain the pasta and toss with the Parmesan cheese first; then toss the sauce through the pasta.

Linguine with zucchini and leeks

 About 1 hour

Calories per portion: 385

Freisa secco d'Asti (Piedmont) (red)

For four: *¹/₂ pound linguine (4" long) - 1 pound fresh zucchini - 1 pound fresh leeks - 9 cups of chicken broth - 4 tablespoons butter - 1 clove of garlic - 4 tablespoons chopped parsley - pinch of cinnamon - salt and pepper - grated Parmesan cheese.*

Instructions: Wash and dice the leeks, zucchini, parsley, and the garlic; saute in butter for 15 minutes; then cover and simmer with a small amount of broth for an additional ten minutes; add the cinnamon and the remainder of the broth and bring to a boil. Add the pasta and sprinkle with the parsley; cook the pasta until firm to the bite and serve in warm bowls with Parmesan cheese on the top.

Assi di quadri with spinach

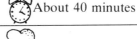 About 40 minutes

Calories per portion: 190

Terlaner bianco (Trentino-Alto Adige) (white)

For four: *¹/₂ pound assi di quadri - ¹/₂ pound fresch spinach - ¹/₂ cup fresh or frozen peas - 8 cups chicken or vegetable broth - Parmesan cheese - salt.*

Instructions: Cook peas in the broth. Wash and cut the spinach into small strips. When the peas are almost ready, add the spinach and cook, for 10 minutes. Add the pasta and cook for 2-3 minutes, serve in warm bowls with the grated cheese on top.

57

Tagliatelle medie

Also called Small Fettuccine
Recommended kind of dough: With eggs
Cooking time: 5 minutes
To be used: Drained (4 ounces per portion)
Variation: Quadrucci. To be used for soups with meat, chicken or vegetable broths. Cut the tagliatelle medie lengthwise into 1/4" long pieces.

Tagliatelle with "harmony sauce"

 About 2 hours

Calories per portion: 698

 Castel del Monte rosato (Apulia) (rosé)

For four: 1 pound tagliatelle medie - 6 tablespoons butter - 1 small red pepper - 1 small yellow sweet pepper - 3 to 4 plum tomatoes - 2 small cucumbers - 1 medium size onion - 1/4 cup chopped Italian parsley - 3 fresh basil leaves (or 1/4 teaspoon dried basil) - 1 fresh fennel (Italian celery) - 1 medium size zucchini - 1 carrot - 2 stalks of celery - 4 tablespoons olive oil - 1/2 cup dry white wine - 1/2 cup dry Martini & Rossi Vermouth (or dry Sherry) - 2 tablespoons vinegar - 2 tablespoons Worcester sauce - grated Parmesan cheese.

Instructions: Wash and chop the vegetables; saute in the butter until semi-soft, then pour in the white wine, vinegar, and dry Martini & Rossi with the Worcester sauce - cook over low heat, covered, for one hour. Cook and drain the pasta and toss with butter and grated Parmesan cheese, then toss with the vegetable sauce. Serve immediately.

Tagliatelle "Spring style"

 About 50 minutes

Calories per portion: 821

 Chianti dei Colli Fiorentini (Tuscany) aged 1-2 years (red)

For four: 1 pound tagliatelle medie - 6 tablespoons butter - 1/4 pound ham (1 thick slice) - 1 cup shelled peas - 1/2 teaspoon sugar - 1 cup cream - grated Parmesan cheese - pepper.

Instructions: Cut the ham into small cubes and saute in the butter for a few minutes; boil the peas until cooked, yet firm in boiling water with the sugar. Add the peas to the ham with 3 tablespoons of the cooking water and allow to cook for ten minutes; pour in the cream, stir, and allow the cream to thicken (4-5 minutes). Sprinkle with freshly ground pepper. Cook and drain the pasta and toss with the Parmesan cheese and then the sauce. Serve immediately.

Tagliatelle with "harmony sauce"

Tagliatelle "Spring style"

Tagliatelle "bacon sauce"

  About 20 minutes

Calories per portion: 795

 Colli del Trasimeno rosso (Umbria) (red)

For four: 1 pound tagliatelle medie - ¹/₄ pound bacon - 4 tablespoons of butter - ¹/₂ cup cream - grated Parmesan cheese - salt and pepper.

Instructions: Slice the bacon into small strips and saute in a large frying pan with the butter until browned. Cook and drain the pasta and transfer to the frying pan and toss with the bacon sauce. Add the cream and Parmesan cheese and toss through, adding the freshly ground black pepper. Serve immediately.

Tagliatelle omelette "Calabrian style" (frittata)

  About 30 minutes

Calories per portion: 455

Aglianico dei Colli Lucani (Basilicata) aged 1 year (red)

For four: ¹/₂ pound tagliatelle medie - 6 eggs - ¹/₄ pound mozzarella cheese - 4 slices salami - 7 fresh basil leaves - ¹/₂ cup milk - 4 tablespoons of butter - dash of cinnamon powder - salt.

Instructions: Cook and drain the tagliatelle until firm to the bite (you can use leftover tagliatelle, provided they have not been dressed with the sauce). Transfer to a mixing bowl; mix the eggs in a separate bowl with the milk and cinnamon; beat for 5 minutes, toss the egg mixture through the pasta. Dice the mozzarella cheese, salami, and basil leaves and add to the mixing bowl and toss through. Melt the butter in a non-stick frying pan and add the mixture; cook the bottom side until golden brown; then place a dish on top and turn the mixture into a dish, then return to the pan and cook the other side until golden brown. Serve immediately cutting the omelette into pie-size pieces. (You can serve with cheese or tomato sauce on top). (This is the Italian version of the omelette that is flat like a pie and cooked on both sides, called "Frittata").

Tagliatelle pie

  About 1½ hours

Calories per portion: 549

Asti Spumante (Piedmont) (white)

For six: *for noodles - ½ pound flour in the PastaMatic measuring cup - 2 eggs - dash of vanilla - salt. For pie: 3½ ounces almonds - 2 ounces walnuts - 2 ounces pine nuts - 2 ounces hazel nuts - 5 ounces macaroons - 1 cup sugar - 6 tablespoons butter - 4 eggs - ½ cup rum - 1 grated and peeled lemon - 3 tablespoons powder sugar - 2 tablespoons flour.*

Instructions: Grease a large baking pan with butter and sprinkle with flour; mash all the nuts, finely and the macaroons; mix eggs, rum and lemon together. Preheat oven to 350° F. Prepare the tagliatelle noodles as usual but add the vanilla; layer the bottom of the baking pan with 1/3 of the noodles; add a sprinkling of the macaroons and the nuts. Repeat, alternating the layers of noodles and nut mixture to the top of the pan; pour the egg, rum, lemon peel mixture over the top of the pie. Bake the pie for 45 minutes 350 °F, until the top becomes a rich golden color. Before serving, sprinkle the powder sugar on the top. Serve hot or cold.

Quadrucci soup with peas

  About 1 hour

Calories per portion: 400

Trebbiano di Romagna (Romagna) (white)

For four: *½ pound quadrucci - 1 small onion - 1 tablespoon butter - 1 pound fresh peas - 10 cups broth (chicken, vegetable or beef) or stock cubes can be used with water - 2 egg yolks - 2 ounces grated Parmesan cheese - ¼ pound ham - salt.*

Instructions: Chop the onion and saute in the butter until golden brown; add the shelled peas and stir-cook 4-5 minutes. Pour in the broth and add the salt; cook 20 minutes; add the pasta and cook 5 minutes. Add the egg yolks, cheese and diced ham to a mixing bowl and blend thoroughly; pour into the soup and stir through. Serve immediately; more cheese can be added to the top.

Tagliatelle

Also called Fettuccine
Recommended kind of dough: With eggs - with whole-wheat flour - with durum wheat flour
Cooking time: 5 minutes - 8 minutes - 6 minutes
To be used: Drained (4 ounces per portion)

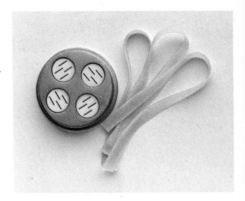

Tagliatelle "sea style"

 About 40 minutes

Calories per portion: 576

 Pigato di Albenga (Liguria) (white)

For four: *1 pound tagliatelle - ¹/₄ cup olive oil - 3 cloves garlic - 1 small chili pepper - 4 flat anchovy fillets - 10 peeled plum tomatoes (canned) - 10 green olives - 10 black olives - 1 tablespoon capers.*

Instructions: Chop the garlic, chili pepper, and olives; mash the anchovy fillets and slice the tomatoes. Saute the garlic and chili pepper in the oil for a few minutes; remove the chili pepper and add the anchovies, stir and cook a few minutes. Remove from the heat and add the tomatoes, olives, and capers and cook over medium heat for 15-20 minutes. Cook and drain the pasta. Pour the sauce and toss through the pasta.

Tagliatelle with German sauce

 About 30 minutes

Calories per portion: 565

 Casteller (Trentino-Alto Adige) (red)

For four: *1 pound tagliatelle - 3 skinned Würstel pork sausages - ¹/₄ cup chopped parsley - 4 tablespoons butter - dash of paprika - 1 teaspoon corn flour - 1 cup cream - grated Parmesan cheese - salt.*

Instructions: Slice the pork sausages and heat them in the foaming butter. After 5 minutes, add the washed, finely chopped parsley (if you own the BravoSimac it takes only 30 seconds). Melt the corn flour with the cream and pour over the sausages. Season with the paprika and salt and bring to a boil. Cook and drain the pasta and pour the sauce over the pasta and toss through. Sprinkle with the cheese.

Tagliatelle with German sauce

Baked tagliatelle with anchovies and mozzarella

 About 50 minutes

Calories per portion: 693

 Gragnano Rosso (Campania) aged 1 year (red)

For four: *1 pound tagliatelle - 4 tablespoons butter - ¹/₂ pound mozzarella cheese - 4 tablespoons grated Parmesan cheese - 6 flat anchovy fillets - salt and pepper.*

Instructions: Finely slice the mozzarella cheese and cut the anchovy fillets into small pieces; cook and drain the pasta - cooking only half the time very firm.
Toss with melted butter and line the bottom of a pre-greased (with butter) baking pan, using only half the noodles. Sprinkle the mozzarella cheese slices on top with the anchovy pieces and the grated cheese. Make another line of pasta, cheese, and anchovies; top with Parmesan cheese and bake at 400 °F for 15 minutes.

Fettuccine "naïf style"

 About 25 minutes

Calories per portion: 580

 Cerasuolo di Abruzzo (Abruzzo) (white)

For four: *1 pound fettuccine - 15 black olives - 6 green olives - 1 cup canned tuna fish (water packed) - ¹/₄ pound corned tongue - 8 fresh basil leaves - 1 teaspoon grated orange peel - 4 tablespoons olive oil - salt and pepper.*

Instructions: Chop and pit the olives; grate the orange peel; dice the tongue and mash the tuna fish.
Cook and drain the fettuccine and rinse in cold water to stop the cooking process; toss with the olive oil, olives, tongue, tuna, diced basil leaves, orange peel and salt and pepper. Mix the sauce through and serve immediately.

Fettuccine with Marsala ragu sauce

   About 1 hour and 15 minutes

Calories per portion: 747

Bonarda dell'Oltrepò Pavese (Lombardy) (red)

For four: 1 pound fettuccine - 2 cloves garlic - ¹/₂ teaspoon rosemary - ¹/₂ cup tomato puree - ¹/₂ cup dry Marsala wine - 4 tablespoons olive oil - 4 tablespoons butter - pinch of cinnamon powder - grated Parmesan cheese - ¹/₂ pound minced veal or beef - salt and pepper.

Instructions: Chop the garlic and saute with the rosemary in the butter and oil a few minutes; add the meat and stir constantly - just cook until the meat turns brown - season with cinnamon, salt and pepper; pour in the Marsala wine and cook for ten minutes over low heat. Mix the tomato puree with two tablespoons water and stir until smooth; add to the meat mixture and cook down for about 40 minutes.
Cook and drain the pasta; toss with the cheese and the meat sauce; add more cheese before serving.

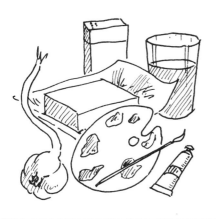

Tagliatelle with saffron and curry

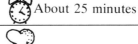 About 25 minutes

Calories per portion: 445

Sangiovese delle Rocche di Predappio (Romagna) (red)

For four: 1 pound tagliatelle - 4 tablespoons of butter - ¹/₂ cup cream - 1 teaspoon curry powder - ¹/₂ teaspoon saffron - salt and pepper.

Instructions: Heat the curry powder and the saffron in the butter, 2-3 minutes; add the cream and salt and allow to simmer 4-5 minutes. Cook and drain the pasta and transfer to a large heated serving bowl and toss the sauce through. Serve immediately.

Pappardelle

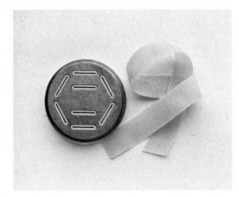

Also called Wide Fettuccine
Recommended kind of dough: With eggs - with whole-wheat flour - with durum wheat flour
Cooking time: 8 minutes - 10 minutes - 7 minutes
To be used: Drained (4 ounces per portion)
Variation: Farfalle (butterflies). To be used drained. Cut pasta lenghtwise into 1" long pieces and squeeze each piece in the middle.

Pappardelle with mushroom sauce

  About 1 hour and 30 minutes

Calories per portion: 570

Dolcetto d'Alba (Piedmont) aged 1 year (red)

For four: 1 pound tagliatelle - ¹/₂ cup dried, wild mushrooms - ¹/₄ cup olive oil - 4 tablespoons butter - 1 small onion - 2 cloves garlic - ¹/₂ cup milk - pinch cinnamon powder - grated Parmesan cheese - salt and pepper.

Instructions: Soak the mushrooms in cold water for 30 minutes; chop the onion and the garlic. Saute the onion and garlic with the mushrooms for about 45 minutes (in oil and butter), gradually adding the milk and cinnamon and salt and pepper to taste. Cook and drain the pasta and toss with the Parmesan cheese; then the sauce. Add more cheese as you toss through.

Farfalle with salmon sauce

  About 25 minutes

Calories per portion: 598

Sylvaner dell'Alto Adige (Trentino-Alto Adige) (white)

For four: 1 pound farfalle - 1 pound peeled plum tomatoes - ¹/₄ pound smoked salmon - 4 tablespoons butter - 1 clove of garlic - pinch of cinnamon powder - 1 cup cream - salt and pepper.

Instructions: Wash and dice the tomatoes; dice the garlic and the salmon into short strips. Heat the garlic in the oil a few minutes; then discard. Add the tomatoes and cook for 10 minutes. Stir through the tomatoes, the strips of salmon and season with cinnamon powder and salt; simmer for 15 minutes. While the sauce is cooking, boil the water and cook and drain the pasta; toss with the cream and then the tomato-salmon sauce. Sprinkle fresh ground pepper on the top and serve immediately.

Tagliatelle with mushroom sauce

Farfalle with salmon sauce

Pappardelle with "hare meat sauce"

   About 1½ hours

Calories per portion: 736

Chianti delle Colline Pisane (Tuscany) (red)

For four: 1 pound pappardelle - 1 pound of ground wild game meat (or rabbit) - 4 tablespoons of butter - ¼ pound of pancetta (slab bacon or prosciutto can be used) - 1 medium size onion - 1 stalk celery - 1 carrot - 2 bayleaves - 1 tablespoon potato flour - 1 cup dry red wine - ½ cup broth - Parmesan cheese - salt and pepper.

Instructions: Chop the pancetta, onion, celery, carrot and bayleaf and saute in the butter for 5-8 minutes; add the wild game meat, salt and pepper, stir through and cook until browned. Add the potato flour thinned with the wine and cook down for about 10 minutes. Add the broth and simmer over low heat for 35 minutes. Cook and drain the pasta and toss with the meat sauce and sprinkle with Parmesan cheese.

Pappardelle with duck sauce

   About 2 hours

Calories per portion: 757

Carmignano (Tuscany) aged 1 year (red)

For four: 1 pound pappardelle - 1 small young duck - duck giblets - ¼ pound pancetta (thick bacon) - 3 ounces olive oil - 1 medium size onion - 1 carrot - 1 stalk celery - 1 clove garlic - 3 tablespoons chopped parsley - 2 to 3 sage leaves - 1 bayleaf - 1 cup dry white wine - 1 cup tomato puree - ½ cup milk - grated Parmesan cheese - salt and pepper.

Instructions: Chop the onion, celery, carrot, pancetta, parsley, sage, bayleaf, and giblets; saute the pancetta in the oil with the sage and bayleaf; after 5 minutes, add the giblets. Wash and cut the duck into small pieces; saute the duck pieces with the pancetta mixture until golden brown. Pour small amounts of wine as the duck is cooking; add salt and pepper; when entire wine amount has cooked for 15 minutes add the tomato puree, thinned with the milk; stir through and cook for 10 minutes (covered). Remove the duck pieces and allow the sauce to thicken, cooking an additional 10 minutes. Cook and drain the pasta, toss with the Parmesan cheese and toss the duck sauce through the pasta. Use the duck pieces as a second course, warmed with ¼ cup of dry wine; cook down 5-8 minutes.

Pizzoccheri

  About 1 hour and 15 minutes

Calories per portion: 551

Inferno Valtellina Superiore
(Lombardy) (red)

*For four: dough: ¹/₂ pound all purpose
flour, measured in the PastaMatic cup - ¹/₂
pound buckwheat flour, measured in the
PastaMatic cup - 4 large eggs measured in
the PastaMatic liquid measuring cup to
mark for 1 pound of flour.
Sauce: 7 ounces mozzarella or fontina
cheese - 2 ounces butter - 3-4 sage leaves - 2
cloves garlic - 3 medium size potatoes - ¹/₂
pound cabbage leaves - grated Parmesan
cheese - salt and pepper.*

Instructions: Make the dough with the
eggs - use appropriate disc and cut the
dough lengthwise into 3" pieces (pizzoccheri) and spread over flat surface to dry,
sprinkle with plain flour. Peel and chop
the potatoes and cabbage; cook potatoes
in boiling water for 10 minutes, then add
the cabbage and cook for 10 more minutes;
add the pizzoccheri and cook for 5
minutes more. Saute the chopped garlic in
butter with the diced sage leaves for a few
minutes. Dice the cheese - drain pasta and
vegetables - toss with the cheese strips,
garlic-sage sauce, Parmesan cheese, salt
and pepper. Alternate layers of cheese-
coated pizzoccheri with the vegetables.
Serve hot.

Pizzoccheri with red sauce

  About 1 hour and 20 minutes

Calories per portion: 921

Sassella della Valtellina
(Lombardy) aged 2 years (red)

*For four: 1 pound pizzoccheri - ¹/₄ cup
olive oil - 1 small onion - 1 carrot - 1 stalk
celery - ¹/₂ pound ground beef meat - 1 cup
red wine - ¹/₂ pound peeled plum tomatoes -
1 cup beef-broth - grated Parmesan cheese
- salt and pepper.*

Instructions: Prepare the vegetables:
wash and chop the onion, carrot, celery,
and tomatoes. Saute in the oil for 5 to 8
minutes; add the meat and stir while the
meat cooks for 5 minutes; add the wine
and cook 15 minutes.
Stir in the tomatoes and cook for 40 minutes,
gradually adding the broth to thin the
sauce; season with salt and pepper.
Cook and drain the pasta, sprinkle and
toss with the grated cheese and add the
sauce and toss through. Serve immediately.

Sfoglie

Also called Lasagne
Recommended kind of dough: With eggs
Cooking time: about 8 minutes

Chiacchiere

 About 1 hour and 15 minutes

Calories per portion: 421

Gran Spumante Corvo amabile (Sicily) (white)

For four: 1 pound flour, measured in the PastaMatic cup - 1 egg - 3 ounces sugar - 3 ounces milk - ¹/₂ cup grappa liqueur - 1 tablespoon seed oil - 3 to 4 cups vegetable oil-powder sugar.

Instructions: Put flour and sugar in the PastaMatic bowl and turn the machine on; after a few minutes pour in the eggs and the milk with the appropriate measuring cup through the opening in the lid; add the grappa liqueur and the seed oil and allow to knead for 5 more minutes. Turn off the PastaMatic and allow to set for 30 minutes; remove the slide so that some dough is extruded and fix the appropriate disc (which must be preheated in hot water) to the face of the machine. Cut the dough lengthwise into 4" pieces and saute two or three at one time in abundant hot oil (oil must not be too hot or the chiacchiere will not swell). Drain when they become a golden color and dry them on paper towels. Sprinkle with powder sugar.

Baked green pasta with mozzarella cheese

 About 45 minutes - plus time for Bechamel sauce

Calories per portion: 632

Rosso dei Colli dèl Trasimeno (Umbria) (red)

For four: 1 pound pasta strips (see instructions for spinach pasta on page 158), cut lengthwise into 5" strips - ¹/₂ pound mozzarella cheese - ¹/₄ cup grated Parmesan cheese - 4 tablespoons butter.
Bechamel sauce: ¹/₄ cup plain flour - 4 tablespoon butter - 3 cups milk - dash of nutmeg - salt and pepper (as instructed on page 72 "Baked Lasagne").

Instructions: Add the pasta strips to rapidly boiling water; add 1 tablespoon of olive oil to keep the pasta strips from sticking together; cook for 5 minutes; drain the pasta strips and lay them on a slightly wet kitchen cloth. Grease a rectangular pan with butter and cover the bottom of the pan with a layer of pasta; spread a small amount of bechamel over the pasta strips; then mozzarella cheese strips and grated Parmesan cheese. Alternate the layers of pasta, sauce and cheese to the top of the pan. Bake at 350 °F for 15 minutes.

Baked lasagne

 About 1 hour, plus time to prepare the ragu sauce.

Calories per portion: 703

Albana amabile di Romagna (Emilia-Romagna) (red)

For four: 1 pound pasta strips (cut the egg dough lengthwise into 5" strips).
Ragu meat sauce: (as instructed on page 50) - 4 tablespoons grated Parmesan cheese - 2 tablespoons butter - ¼ cup fine breadcrumbs - 1 tablespoon olive oil.
Bechamel sauce: 4 tablespoons butter - ¼ cup plain flour - 3 cups milk - pinch of nutmeg - salt and pepper.

Instructions: Cook the strips of pasta in rapidly boiling water, adding a small amount of olive oil; drain the strips of pasta and lay over a slightly wet kitchen cloth to dry out; prepare the ragu sauce as instructed on page 50; while the sauce is cooking, make the bechamel sauce: thin the plain flour in a small bowl with the milk; add the rest of the milk and butter and heat the mixture stirring constantly until the sauce has thickened and starts to bubble; add salt and pepper and nutmeg and cook another 10 minutes. Grease the heat-resistant rectangular pan with some butter and spread a small amount of ragu sauce over the bottom; lay some cooked pasta strips across the bottom then more ragu sauce then bechamel sauce on top of the ragu sauce. Sprinkle with some grated cheese and alternate layers of pasta, ragu and bechamel sauce until completed; top with bechamel sauce and grated cheese - then finely grated breadcrumbs and small pieces of butter. Bake at 350 °F until the top has turned brown and crispy; about 8 to 10 minutes.

Baked pasta with ricotta cheese and ham

 About 2 hours

Calories per portion: 932

Villa Banfi Frascati (Latium) (white)

For four: 3/4 pound strips of pasta - (cut into 5" lengths) - 1 tablespoon olive oil - ½ pound mozzarella cheese - ¼ pound ham - 1 cup ricotta cheese - 4 tablespoons grated Parmesan cheese - 2 eggs - pinch of nutmeg - 1 tablespoon parsley.
Tomato sauce: 2 tablespoons butter - 1 small onion - 2 cups tomato puree - 7 basil leaves - grated Parmesan cheese.

Instructions: Cook the strips of pasta (a few at a time) in rapidly boiling water (adding a small amount of olive oil), stirring to keep the strips from sticking; drain the pasta strips and lay them over a slightly wet kitchen cloth to dry. Dice the mozzarella cheese and cut the ham into small strips; crush the ricotta cheese with a fork and add the mozzarella cheese and ham; mix through the eggs and grated cheese, nutmeg, chopped parsley, salt and pepper. Grease a heat-resistant baking pan with butter; layer the bottom of the pan with the pasta strips; slightly overlapping. Pour a small amount of the cheese - ham sauce over the pasta strips. Make the tomato sauce: add the diced onion to the butter and saute a minute; then add the tomatoes and allow to cook for 10 minutes; add the diced basil leaves the last few minutes. Add another layer of pasta strips to the baking pan and top with the tomato sauce; alternate the cheese-ham sauce on one layer and the tomato sauce on the other. Top with the grated cheese and bake for 15 minutes at 350 °F, until golden brown and bubbling.

Cannelloni delle Langhe

 About 1 hour and 20 minutes

Calories per portion: 1075

 Dolcetto d'Asti (Piedmont) (red)

For four: *1 pound of pasta strips, 3" long - 1 pound of diced chicken breast meat (preboiled) - ¼ pound of ham - ½ cup diced soft bread soaked in ½ cup milk - 4 egg yolks - 2 egg whites - 4 tablespoons grated Parmesan cheese - pinch of grated nutmeg - 4 tablespoons olive oil - salt and pepper. Topping: 4 tablespoons butter - 5 ounces Italian fontina cheese.*

Instructions: Boil, then chop the chicken very fine: dice the ham and add the bread to the milk and squeeze out excess and cut into pieces. Add all of the above ingredients in a large bowl and mix thoroughly; beat the egg whites and gently fold through the mixture and add the grated cheese, nutmeg, salt and pepper and blend through; set aside. Cook the pasta strips - a few at a time in boiling water, adding a small amount of olive oil, and drain - dry on a kitchen cloth; spread a small amount of stuffing mixture on each strip of pasta and roll up on the narrow side, obtaining a short "cannelloni" shape. Grease a baking pan with butter and lay the cannelloni side by side; add small pieces of butter and thin slices of fontina cheese. If necessary, make two layers of cannelloni. Bake at 350 °F until the top becomes crisp and golden colored.

Fried pasta strips with cheese

 About 25 minutes

Calories per portion: 336

 Vernaccia di San Gimignano (Tuscany) (white)

For four: *½ pound all-purpose flour (measured in the PastaMatic measuring cup) - 4 tablespoons grated Parmesan cheese - 1 cup lukewarm water up to the level mark for ½ pound of flour on the PastaMatic liquid measuring cup - ½ cup vegetable oil and your choice of: anchovies, ham, salami or sausage, melting cheese.*

Instructions: Pour the flour and Parmesan cheese into the PastaMatic bowl; allow to knead for a few minutes and add the lukewarm water, using the liquid measuring cup for the PastaMatic. Allow the dough to knead for 5 minutes; remove the slide and allow some dough to be extruded. Turn the PastaMatic off, fasten the disc into place, which should be preheated in hot water. Cut the dough lengthwise into 2" strips. Heat the vegetable oil until hot - fry the dough - turning the strips on the other side, and remove as they turn golden brown. Dry the strips on paper towels and serve hot.

Variation: cut the dough lengthwise into 4" pieces and fold them into halves; stuff with anchovy or ham, salami, or cheese. Press the borders and dry as instructed; serve hot. Great as an appetizer or with cocktails.

Bucatini *(hollow spaghetti)*

Recommended kind of dough: With eggs - with whole-wheat flour - with durum wheat flour
Cooking time: 5 minutes - 7 minutes - 4 minutes
To be used: Drained (4 ounces per portion)
Variation: Ave Marie. To be used in meat or vegetable broth. Cut pasta lenghtwise into 1/8" long pieces.

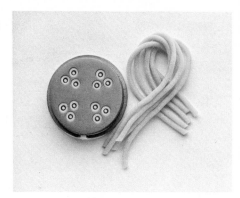

Bucatini alla amatriciana

 About 1 hour

Calories per portion: 773

 Torgiano rosso (Umbria) aged 1-2 years (red)

For four: 1 pound bucatini - 3 tablespoons olive oil - ¹/₂ pound bacon (cut in single slice) - 2 cloves of garlic - 1 medium onion - ¹/₄ teaspoon Italian herb seasoning - ¹/₂ cup red wine - 1 pound peeled plum tomatoes - 2 teaspoons tomato paste - salt and pepper - grated Romano cheese.

Instructions: Dice the bacon, onion, garlic and tomatoes. Saute the bacon in the oil until translucent; add the chopped garlic and onion and saute for 5 minutes; add the Italian herb seasoning and wine and cook for 5 to 8 minutes. Add the tomatoes, peeled and diced, with the tomato paste, pepper and salt. Cook over low heat for 30 minutes, stirring frequently.
Cook the bucatini and drain. Toss with the Romano cheese and toss with the sauce. Serve immediately.

Bucatini with artichoke and pea sauce

 About 50 minutes

Calories per portion: 735

 Verdicchio dei Castelli di Jesi (Marche) (white)

For four: 1 pound bucatini - 1 small onion - 1 clove garlic - 4 tablespoons butter - 2 tablespoons olive oil - a pinch of cinnamon powder - 3 small artichokes - ¹/₂ pound shelled peas - ¹/₂ cup cream - grated Parmesan cheese - 4 tablespoons Italian parsley - salt and pepper.

Instructions: Chop the onion, garlic, and parsley; saute the onion and garlic in the butter and oil for a few minutes; prepare the artichokes by snapping off the leaves and keeping the tender part only. Slice the artichokes very finely and mix in with the peas, salt and pepper with a dash of cinnamon powder, and saute with the onion-garlic mixture for 5 to 8 minutes. Add the cream and parsley and blend through.
Cook and drain the pasta, toss with the sauce and sprinkle with the grated cheese. Serve immediately.

74

Bucatini with fresh tomato sauce

  About 25 minutes

Calories per portion: 595

Episcopio rosato (Campania) (rosé)

For four: 1 pound bucatini - 6 tablespoons olive oil - 2 cloves of garlic - 8 plum tomatoes - small chili pepper - 12 basil leaves - salt and pepper.

Instructions: Dice the garlic and chili pepper; saute in the oil for a few minutes, discard; add the peeled and diced tomatoes and cook for 6 to 8 minutes; add the diced basil leaves, salt and pepper and stir through. Cook for 2 minutes. Cook and drain the pasta and toss with the tomato sauce.

Bucatini "mazzarese style"

  About 15 minutes

Calories per portion: 695

Belice rosso (Sicily) (red)

For four: 1 pound bucatini - 20 black olives - 6 tablespoons olive oil - 1 clove garlic - 8 fresh basil leaves - 1 tablespoon pine nuts - 3/4 cup cream - salt and pepper.

Instructions: Remove the stones from the olives and put into a food processor, adding the oil and pine nuts. Mince and pour the mixture into a small frying pan. Heat a few minutes with the cream and chopped garlic; allow to simmer for 5 minutes. Cook and drain the pasta; toss with the sauce and add the diced basil leaves and toss through. Serve immediately.

Bucatini with simple mushroom sauce

 About 1 hour

Calories per portion: 525

 Collio Sauvignon (Friuli-Venezia Giulia) (white)

For four: 1 pound bucatini - ¹/₂ pound fresh mushrooms - 4 tablespoons butter - 1 clove garlic - 1 tablespoon parsley - ¹/₂ cup cream - 1 tablespoon lemon juice - grated Parmesan cheese - pinch cinnamon powder.

Instructions: Prepare and slice the mushrooms; chop the garlic, parsley and grate the Parmesan cheese. Saute the garlic in the butter and add the sliced mushrooms, cinnamon powder and salt; allow to cook for about 30 minutes. Pour in the cream and stir constantly, for 5 to 8 minutes. Mix in the parsley and lemon juice. Cook and drain the pasta and toss with the Parmesan cheese, then the sauce.

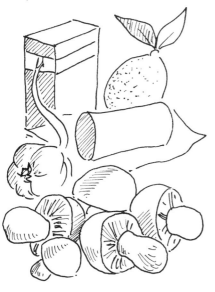

Ave Marie with vegetables

 About 45 minutes

Calories per portion: 513

 Bianco Vergine della Val Chiana (Tuscany) (white)

For four: ¹/₂ pound Ave Marie - 4 leeks - 2 potatoes - 2 bayleaves - 4 tablespoons butter - 4 tablespoons olive oil - pinch grated nutmeg - 9 cups broth (stock cubes can be used) - 2 ounces fontina cheese - 2 ounces Italian ricotta cheese - grated Parmesan cheese - salt and pepper.

Instructions: Slice the leeks (also the tender green part), peel and chop the potatoes. Crush the bayleaves and dice the fontina cheese. Saute the vegetables in the butter and oil with the bayleaves, nutmeg and seasoning. Stir frequently for about 5 to 8 minutes. Add the broth and cook for 20 minutes. After the broth comes to an immediate boil, drop in the Ave Marie and cook until firm to the bite. Add some pepper, the ricotta cheese, and sliced fontina cheese and grated Parmesan cheese. Stir, cover and allow to set about 5 minutes.

Bucati rigati
(hollow ridged spaghetti)

Recommended kind of dough: With eggs - with whole-wheat flour - with durum wheat flour
Cooking time: 5-8 minutes - 12 minutes - 10 minutes
To be used: Drained (4 ounces per portion)
Variation: Ditali rigati. To be used for vegetable soups. Cut the pasta lengthwise into ½" long pieces.

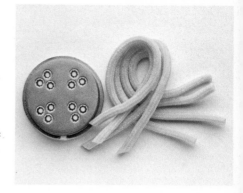

Bucati rigati "lampara style"

 About 15 minutes

Calories per portion: 544

 Trebbiano d'Abruzzo (Abruzzo) (white)

For four: *1 pound bucati rigati - 4 tablespoons olive oil - 1 clove garlic - 1 lemon - 3 tablespoons parsley - 5 ounces tuna fish (canned without oil) - 2 flat anchovy fillets - 2 to 4 drops Tabasco sauce - salt.*

Instructions: Chop the garlic, and parsley; mash the anchovy fillets and mix with the garlic and Tabasco sauce and oil. Mash the tuna fish with the lemon juice. Cook and drain the pasta, toss with the sauce and add the tuna fish-lemon juice mixture and toss through. Add the parsley and toss again.

Bucati rigati with shrimp "Torcello style"

 About 30 minutes

Calories per portion: 527

 Pinot grigio delle Grave del Friuli (Friuli-Venezia Giulia) (white)

For four: *1 pound bucati rigati - 5 ounces shelled shrimp - 1 clove garlic - 4 plum tomatoes - 3 tablespoons parsley - pinch of ginger - ½ cup of dry white wine - ¼ cup olive oil - salt and pepper.*

Instructions: Chop the garlic, tomatoes, and parsley. Saute the garlic in the oil a few minutes, then discard. Add the shelled shrimp and season with the ginger, stir and cook about 5 minutes. Add the wine and cook a few minutes, then add the tomatoes and cook for 3 to 5 minutes (not longer or the shrimp will become tough). Cook and drain the pasta and toss with the sauce. Sprinkle with the chopped parsley and toss. Serve immediately.

78

Bucati rigati with shrimp "Torcello style"

Ditali rigati with zucchini

 About 1 hour

Calories per portion: 431

 Merlot del Montello Rosato (Venetia) (rosé)

For four: *½ pound ditali rigati - 4 tablespoons butter - 1 tablespoon grated nutmeg - 1 small onion - 1 pound fresh zucchini - 2 cloves garlic - 3 cups milk - pinch of sugar - 1 stock cube - grated Romano cheese - 1 cup water - salt and pepper (stock cube may be either chicken or vegetable).*

Instructions: Chop the onion, garlic, and zucchini. Saute the onion in the butter and oil until golden brown. Cook the zucchini with the milk, add the water and garlic and press through a food mill or sieve to obtain a puree.
Mix the zucchini puree with the onion and cook a few minutes; add the stock cube, sugar and salt and cook for 15-20 minutes (add more water to make the soup texture if you prefer).
Bring to a boil and add the pasta; cook for 10 minutes stirring frequently. Serve with fresh ground pepper and grated Romano cheese on top.

Bucati rigati with fresh vegetables

 About 25 minutes

Calories per portion: 580

 Marzemino di Isera (Trentino) (red)

For four: *1 pound bucati rigati - 2 cloves of garlic - 3-4 chive leaves (or use dry chives, ½ teaspoon) - 8 basil leaves (or ½ teaspoon dried basil) - 4-5 sage leaves (¼ teaspoon dried sage) - ¼ cup parsley - 1 celery heart - 2 radishes - 4 plum tomatoes - 6 tablespoons olive oil - salt and pepper. (Fresh herbs make a big difference in the taste of this sauce).*

Instructions: Peel and seed the tomatoes, then chop. Chop the vegetables and dice the herbs very fine and transfer to a bowl; add the oil and stir. Cook the pasta and drain. Toss the uncooked sauce and parsley through the pasta and allow to set for a few minutes - covered - then serve.

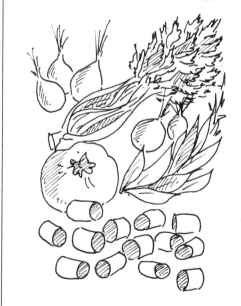

Bucati rigati with pepper sauce

 About 25 minutes

Calories per portion: 570

Corvo di Casteldaccia bianco (Sicily) (white)

For four: *1 pound bucati rigati - 1 large green pepper - 1 large red pepper - 1 large yellow pepper - 1 tablespoon capers - 7 basil leaves - 4 flat anchovy fillets - 2 cloves of garlic - 5 tablespoons olive oil - salt and pepper.*

Instructions: Wash and dry the peppers; char them by placing in a hot oven until crispy brown, or hold with a fork over top of the stove until the skin gets brown; peel the skin and slice into very fine pieces. Add to a bowl with the chopped anchovies and capers, garlic, diced basil leaves salt and pepper and the oil; blend thoroughly. Cook and drain the pasta; toss with the uncooked sauce and allow to sit for a few minutes before serving.

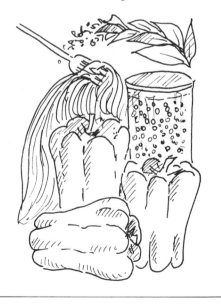

Bucati rigati with mushroom and olive sauce

 About 50 minutes

Calories per portion: 578

Dolcetto di Dogliani (Piedmont) aged 1-2 years (red)

For four: *1 pound bucati rigati - ½ pound fresh mushrooms* - ½ cup black olives - ¼ cup olive oil - 1 clove of garlic - 3 tablespoons Italian parsley - ½ cup dry white wine - salt and pepper - grated Parmesan cheese.*

Instructions: Prepare and slice the mushrooms; chop the garlic and the parsley; saute the garlic in the oil and remove after they become golden in color. Add the mushrooms and cook over a medium heat for 5 minutes; then pour in the wine in small amounts. When the mushrooms are cooked, add the chopped and pitted black olives and saute for 8 minutes, then add the chopped parsley.
Cook and drain the pasta - toss with the Parmesan cheese and then with the sauce.

* Dried mushrooms can be used for a stronger taste: soak in wine for 1 hour before using.

81

Bucati
(large hollow spaghetti)

Recommended kind of dough: With eggs - with whole-wheat flour - with durum wheat flour
Cooking time: 8 minutes - 12 minutes - 10 minutes
To be used: Drained (4 ounces per portion)
Variation: Cannolicchi. To be used for vegetable soups (2 ounces per portion). Cut the pasta lengthwise into 1" long pieces.

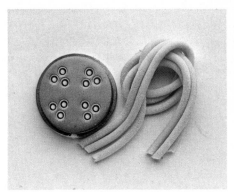

Bucati with pesto sauce

 About 55 minutes

Calories per portion: 746

 Cinque Terre (Liguria) (white)

For four: *1 pound bucati - ¹/₂ pound small potatoes - ¹/₄ cup grated Parmesan cheese - ¹/₂ cup olive oil - 2 cloves garlic - 2 tablespoons pine nuts - about 30 basil leaves - 4 tablespoons water - salt and pepper.*

Instructions: Pesto sauce. Wash, peel and dice the potatoes into ¹/₄ inch pieces, cook for 15 minutes in cold water. Wash and dry the basil leaves and put into a food processor with the oil, water, pine nuts, parsley, and grated cheese, salt and pepper; mince for 1 minute, until the sauce is smooth.
Cook and drain the pasta. Sprinkle with grated cheese and toss with the pesto sauce. Add the diced, cooked potatoes and toss through the pasta and the sauce (if necessary, thin the sauce with some cooking water from the pasta).

Bucati with artichoke sauce

 About 50 minutes

Calories per portion: 570

 Trebbiano di Aprilia (Latium) (white)

For four: *1 pound bucati - 4 artichokes - ¹/₂ cup milk - 2 cloves garlic - ¹/₄ cup Italian parsley - ¹/₂ stock cube (chicken) - 2 tablespoons butter - 4 tablespoons grated Parmesan cheese - 2 egg yolks - ¹/₂ cup cream - salt and pepper.*

Instructions: Snap off the hard, green artichoke leaves and slice the artichoke hearts into very small cubes.
Chop the garlic and saute in the butter with milk and the stock cube and the artichoke cubes until the artichokes become soft. Add the chopped parsley, salt and pepper and stir through. In a mixing bowl add the egg yolks, cream and grated cheese and whip for 3-4 minutes. Cook and drain the pasta; toss with the cream sauce first, then the artichoke sauce. Add more Parmesan cheese and pepper to your taste.

82

Bucati with pesto sauce

Bucati with artichoke sauce

Bucati with black sauce

About 20 minutes

Calories per portion: 592

Bianco dei Colli del Trasimeno (Umbria) (white)

For four: 1 pound bucati - 25 black olives - 6 tablespoons olive oil - 4 flat anchovy fillets - salt and pepper - ¹/₄ cup diced parsley.

Instructions: Remove the stones from the olives and dice them. Wash and chop the parsley; mash the anchovies with the olive oil. Add the olives, parsley, salt and pepper and blend thoroughly.
Cook and drain the pasta; toss with the olive sauce.

Bucati with onions and anchovies

About 45 minutes

Calories per portion: 545

Falerio dei Colli Ascolani (Marche) (white)

For four: 1 pound bucati - ¹/₄ cup olive oil - 1 medium onion - 6 flat anchovy fillets - 4 tablespoons parsley - ¹/₄ teaspoon Italian herb seasoning - salt and pepper - Parmesan cheese.

Instructions: Peel and dice the onion; chop the anchovies and herb seasoning. Saute the onion in the oil until golden brown in color. Add the anchovies, salt and pepper and herb seasoning and cook for 5-8 minutes - until the sauce thickens - add the parsley and stir through.
Cook and drain the pasta, add Parmesan cheese; toss with the sauce.

Bucati with "the improvised sauce"

  About 55 minutes

Calories per portion: 545

Rosatello di Pontassieve (Tuscany) (rosé)

For four: *1 pound bucati - 1 medium onion - ¼ pound small, fresh mushrooms - 10 black olives - 1 tablespoon small capers - ½ cup tomato puree - 3 tablespoons parsley - 4 tablespoons olive oil - ¼ teaspoon Italian herb seasoning - salt and pepper.*

Instructions: Chop the onion, mushrooms and parsley, saute in oil for about 8 minutes, stirring often. Add the olives (diced and pitted), capers and herbs and cook for 6 minutes. Add the tomato puree and simmer for 20 minutes. Season with salt and pepper to taste. Cook and drain the pasta, toss with the sauce and serve immediately.

(You can "improvise" in this sauce by adding your favorite vegetables, or leftover chicken, or turkey).

Cannolicchi soup with pumpkin

  About 40 minutes

Calories per portion: 438

Moltepulciano d'Abruzzo (Abruzzo) aged 1 year (red)

For four: *7 ounces cannolicchi - 20 ounces (net weight) pumpkin - 1 cup shelled peas - 2 leeks - 1 clove of garlic - 2 ounces butter - 2 tablespoons olive oil - 1 ½ cups broth (stock cubes can be used) - salt and pepper - grated Parmesan cheese.*

Instructions: Prepare the vegetables: slice the leeks finely, chop the garlic and cut the pumpkin into small pieces. Fry these ingredients with the peas in the oil and butter. As soon as the vegetables have absorbed the cooking fat, pour in the broth and add salt and pepper. Cook, until done. Add the cannolicchi and simmer. Season with the salt, pepper and top with Parmesan cheese, before serving.

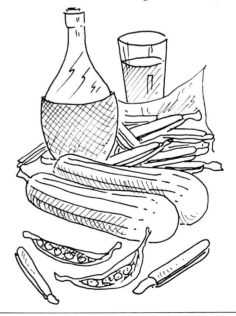

Penne

Also called Ziti

Recommended kind of dough: With whole wheat flour - with durum wheat flour

Cooking time: 7 minutes - 5 minutes

To be used: Drained (4 ounces per portion). Cut the pasta lengthwise into 2" long pieces. The ends must be cut diagonally across.

Variation: Mezze maniche. To be used for vegetable soup or drained with sauces. Cut the pasta lengthwise into 1" long pieces.

Penne with peppers

 About 1 hour

Calories per portion: 661

 Chianti dei Colli Aretini (Tuscany) aged 1-2 years (red)

For four: 1 pound penne - 1 medium onion - ¼ cup olive oil - 4 red peppers (medium size) - 1 cup tomato puree - 10 fresh basil leaves - ½ cup milk - grated Pecorino cheese - ¼ cup chopped parsley - salt and pepper.

Instructions: Slice the onion, peppers and basil leaves; saute in the oil for 8-10 minutes; add the tomato puree and chopped basil leaves and stir constantly. Cook for 20 minutes. Add the chopped parsley and stir through; season with salt and pepper (if the sauce is too thick, thin with water). Cook and drain the pasta; toss with the grated Pecorino cheese first; then the sauce.

Penne "Viterbo style"

 About 20 minutes

Calories per portion: 536

 Orvieto Classico (Umbria) (white)

For four: 1 pound penne - 3 egg yolks - 4 flat anchovy fillets - 2 tablespoons butter - ½ cup diced mozzarella cheese - 3 tablespoons parsley - salt and pepper.

Instructions: Beat the egg yolks with the salt and pepper in a small mixing bowl. Dice the anchovy fillets and the mozzarella cheese and add to the bowl with the parsley and melted butter; blend thoroughly.
Cook and drain the pasta; toss with the sauce. Serve immediately.

Baked penne "Bella Napoli"

Baked penne "Bella Napoli"

 About 1 hour

Calories per portion: 695

Solopaca (Campania) aged 1 year (red) or (white)

For four: 1 pound penne - 4 small eggplants - 2 medium size zucchini - 3 tablespoons plain flour - 2 tablespoons vegetable oil - 2 tablespoons fine bread crumbs - 3 tablespoons butter - 4 tablespoons grated Parmesan cheese - ¼ pound ham - ½ cup diced mozzarella cheese - 2 tablespoons capers - 20 basil leaves.
Tomato sauce: 8 plum tomatoes - 15 basil leaves - 2 tablespoons olive oil.

Instructions: Wash, dry and slice the eggplants and zucchini, then dip the slices in flour and fry them in oil until crisp and golden brown. Grease a heat resistant rectangular pan with butter and sprinkle with bread crumbs and remove the excess. Line the bottom and sides of the pan with the slices of eggplant (not all the slices).
Cook the pasta, keeping it firm and drain. Toss the pasta with butter and grated cheese.
Tomato sauce: peel and dice the tomatoes and place in a food processor with the oil and basil leaves - puree.
Layer the penne over the slices of eggplant in the baking pan, then pieces of ham, mozzarella cheese, zucchini, capers, diced basil leaves and tomato sauce. Alternate the layers of penne, ham and cheese mixture and sauce; at top add some sliced eggplant and tomato sauce with small pieces of butter and a light sprinkling of the fine bread crumbs. Bake at 350 °F for 15 minutes.

"Cala piccola" penne

 About 20 minutes

Calories per portion: 590

Rapitalà (Sicily) (white)

For four: 1 pound penne - ½ cup fine bread crumbs - 5 anchovy fillets - 15 black olives - 1 tablespoon capers - ¼ cup olive oil - salt and pepper - ¼ teaspoon Italian seasoning - 4 tablespoons parsley.

Instructions: Remove the pits from the olives and chop them with the parsley and anchovies. Add part of the oil to a frying pan and saute the anchovies with the capers and olives for 5 minutes. Use the rest of the oil to saute the bread crumbs until golden brown.
Cook and drain the pasta, toss with the bread crumbs first then with the sauce.

Penne "Summer style"

 About 25 minutes

Calories per portion: 760

Ischia rosato (Campania) (rosé)

For four: *1 pound penne - 8 plum tomatoes - 6 tablespoons olive oil - 2 tablespoons capers - 10 basil leaves - ¹/₂ cup shredded mozzarella cheese - 3 tablespoons grated Parmesan cheese - salt and pepper.*

Instructions: Peel and dice the tomatoes, shred the mozzarella cheese and dice the basil leaves. Mix the tomatoes, mozzarella cheese, basil leaves, oil, capers, salt and pepper in a bowl.
Cook and drain the pasta, toss with the Parmesan cheese and with the uncooked sauce.
Cover and allow to set for 10 minutes or longer to let cheese melt.

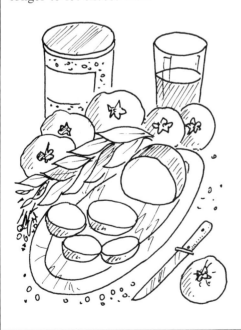

Mezze maniche with mushrooms

 About 45 minutes

Calories per portion: 651

Grignolino d'Asti (Piedmont) aged about 1 year (red)

For four: *1 pound mezze maniche - ¹/₂ pound mushrooms - 6 tablespoons olive oil - 2 cloves of garlic - 1 medium onion - ¹/₂ pound plum tomatoes - 4 tablespoons milk - salt and pepper - 4 tablespoons of parsley - ¹/₄ teaspoon Italian seasoning.*

Instructions: Prepare the mushrooms, slice very fine with the onion, garlic, tomatoes and parsley. Heat the oil and brown the garlic in it, then remove the garlic. Add the onion to the oil and cook until golden brown in color. Add the mushrooms and allow to cook for 5-8 minutes. Add the tomatoes and cook for 20 minutes, adding the milk from time to time.
Season with the salt and herbs and cook for 5 more minutes.
Cook and drain the pasta then toss with the sauce and serve immediately.

Maccheroni

Also called Rigatoni

Recommended kind of dough: With wholewheat flour - with durum wheat flour

Cooking time: Wholewheat flour: 8 minutes - drained 10 minutes - vegetable soup. Durum wheat flour: 6 minutes - drained; 8 minutes - soups.

To be used: Drained (4 ounces per portion). Cut the pasta lengthwise into 2" long pieces.

Variation: Fluted mezze maniche. To be used for vegetable soup - 2 ounces per portion. Cut the pasta lengthwise into 1" long pieces.

Fluted mezze maniche with beans

 About 1 hour and 10 minutes

Calories per portion: 705

 Bardolino Classico (Venetia) (red)

For four: *1/2 pound mezze maniche - 1 pound unshelled, fresh beans - 1 medium onion - 2 cloves garlic - 2 stalks of celery (leaves too) - 3 tablespoons butter - 2 tablespoons olive oil - 1/2 cup milk - 10 cups broth (chicken or beef - stock cube may be used) - 3 tablespoons tomato puree - salt and pepper.*

Instructions: Dice the onion, garlic, and celery; saute in the butter and oil. Add the shelled beans, milk, broth, tomato puree, salt and pepper; allow to cook until the beans are done. In small amounts, add the pasta and stir frequently - until cooked - about 10 minutes.
Sprinkle with pepper and grated cheese, if you like.

Maccheroni with black olive sauce-uncooked

 About 30 minutes

Calories per portion: 502

 Capri bianco (Campania) (white)

For four: *1 pound maccheroni - 4 ounces black olives - 10 fresh basil leaves - 2 tablespoons capers - 3 flat anchovy fillets - 2 eggs - 2 cloves of garlic - 1/4 cup olive oil-salt and pepper.*

Instructions: Boil and shell the eggs; wash and chop the basil leaves; chop and pit the olives; chop the garlic and mash the anchovy fillets. Mix all the ingredients in a large bowl, adding mashed eggs and all of the oil; add salt and pepper to taste. Blend through and allow to set for 15 minutes. Cook and drain the pasta, pour the uncooked sauce over the pasta and toss through.

90

"Marechiaro Maccheroni"

 About 1 hour and 20 minutes

Calories per portion: 541

Ischia rosso (Campania) aged 1 year (red)

For four: *1 pound maccheroni - 1 pound plum tomatoes - 1 clove of garlic - 8 fresh basil leaves - ¼ teaspoon oregano - ½ cup olive oil - 3 tablespoons grated Parmesan cheese - salt and pepper.*

Instructions: Soak the tomatoes in hot water for 2 minutes, remove the skin, then discard the juice and the seeds; chop the tomatoes. Put the tomatoes, oil, oregano, garlic, salt and pepper into a large mixing bowl and blend through; allow to set for 1 hour. Discard the garlic.
Cook and drain the pasta and toss the uncooked sauce through it; add the grated Parmesan cheese and toss again.

Maccheroni with sausage

 About 1 hour

Calories per portion: 861

Valpolicella della Valpantena (Venetia) (red)

For four: *1 pound maccheroni - 1 medium onion - 6 plum tomatoes - 2 tablespoons butter - 3 tablespoons olive oil - ½ pound of sausage - ½ cup milk grated Parmesan cheese - salt.*

Instructions: Chop the onion, garlic and peeled tomatoes. Mash the sausage meat. Saute the onion and garlic in the butter and oil; add the tomatoes and cook for 15 minutes. Mix in the chopped sausage, salt, and cook for 10 minutes, turning often to brown properly. Add the milk slowly and cook for 8 more minutes.
Cook the maccheroni and drain; toss with the cheese then the sauce; blend through the pasta. Serve immediately.

Maccheroni with tuna fish and tomatoes

  About 45 minutes

Calories per portion: 586

Irpinia rosso (Campania) aged 1 year (red)

For four: 1 pound maccheroni - 1 cup tuna fish in oil - 3 tablespoons olive oil - 1 clove garlic - 2 flat anchovy fillets - 1 pound plum tomatoes (canned may be used if drained) - 6 basil leaves (¹/₄ teaspoon of dried basil may be used) - salt and pepper.

Instructions: Add the garlic to the oil and saute for a few minutes; then discard the garlic. Add the anchovy fillets to the oil, mashing with a spoon, then add the tuna fish, which has been drained and mashed, and allow to cook for 5-6 minutes, stirring often. Add the diced tomatoes, diced basil leaves, salt and pepper and cook for 15 minutes.
Cook and drain the pasta and toss with the sauce.

Maccheroni "Gourmet style"

   About 50 minutes

Calories per portion: 665

Aglianico dei Colli Lucani (Basilicata) aged 2 years (red)

For four: 1 pound maccheroni - 4 tablespoons butter - 1 medium onion - ¹/₂ pound mushrooms - ¹/₄ cup dry white wine - ¹/₄ pound ham - 4 tablespoons parsley - 3 tablespoons grated Parmesan cheese - salt and pepper.

Instructions: Dice the onion, mushrooms, ham and parsley. Saute the onion in the butter until golden brown; add the mushrooms, ham and diced parsley, stirring frequently, cook for 15 minutes over a low heat. Add the wine and cook for 8 minutes more.
Cook and drain the pasta and toss first with the grated cheese, then with the sauce.

Pizza

Pizza Margherita

 About 1 hour 30 minutes - plus time for preparing the dough

Calories: 533 per slice

 Belice rosso (Sicily) (red)

For four: For the dough: see the basic pizza dough recipe on page 28.
For the topping: 1 cup diced fresh plum tomatoes or 1 cup tomato sauce - 3 ounces thinly sliced mozzarella cheese - 4 tablespoons olive oil - 6 diced fresh basil leaves (or 1/4 teaspoon dried basil - or use Italian herb seasoning) - salt.

Instructions: Brush the surface of the dough with olive oil. Cover with a kitchen towel and let rise for about 1 hour. Dice the tomatoes, basil leaves, and slice the mozzarella cheese. Heat the oven to 400 °F. Cover the pizza dough with the tomato sauce; sprinkle with cheese then the basil leaves. Bake in the preheated oven for 20-30 minutes, until the crust is brown.

Pizza "Neapolitan style"

 About 1 hour 30 minutes - plus time for preparing the dough

Calories: 560 per slice

 Gragnano (Campania) (red)

For four: For the dough: see basic pizza dough recipe on page 28.
For the topping: 1/2 pound fresh plum tomatoes or 1 cup tomato sauce - 1 cup shredded mozzarella cheese - 8 anchovy fillets - 1/4 teaspoon of Italian herb seasoning - 4 tablespoons olive oil - salt.

Instructions: Brush the surface of the dough with olive oil, cover with a kitchen towel and let rise for 1 hour. Dice the tomatoes, anchovies, and shred the mozzarella. Heat the oven to 400 °F. Spread the tomato sauce over the pizza dough; sprinkle the herb seasoning, diced anchovies and top with the shredded mozzarella cheese. Bake in the preheated oven for 25 minutes, until the crust is golden brown.

Pizza "Capricciosa"

   About 1 hour 20 minutes - plus time for preparing the dough

Calories: 651 per slice

Cesanese del Piglio (Latium) (red)

For four: For the dough: see basic pizza dough recipe on page 28.
For the topping: 1/2 pound mozzarella cheese - 1 tablespoon of capers - 10 black olives - 1/4 pound of fresh mushrooms (or 1/2 cup jarred mushrooms, preserved in oil) - 1/4 pound ham - 4 tablespoons olive oil - 5 small artichoke hearts, in a jar, preserved in oil - 4 tablespoons of Parmesan cheese - salt.

Instructions: Brush the surface of the dough with olive oil; cover with a kitchen towel and let rise for about 1 hour. Dice the mushrooms, artichoke hearts, ham and mozzarella cheese, and pit and chop the olives. Heat the oven to 400 °F. Cover the pizza dough with the mozzarella cheese, ham pieces, mushrooms, artichoke hearts, capers, olives salt and top with the Parmesan cheese. Bake in the preheated oven for 20-30 minutes, until the crust is brown.

Pizza "Marinara"

   About 1 hour 30 minutes - plus time for preparing the dough

Calories: 451 per slice

Ravello rosato (Campania) (rosé)

For four: For the dough: see basic pizza dough recipe on page 28.
For the topping: 1 pound fresh plum tomatoes or 1 cup tomato sauce - 3 cloves of garlic - 6 black olives - pinch of oregano - olive oil - salt.

Instructions: Brush the surface of the pizza dough with the olive oil; cover with a kitchen towel and let rise for 1 hour. Dice the tomatoes, garlic, and pit and chop the olives. Preheat the oven to 400 °F. Cover the pizza dough with the tomatoes, garlic, olives, oregano and salt. Bake for 30 minutes.

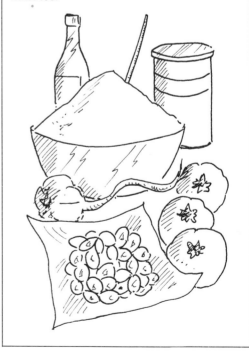

Pizza Sardenaira

  About 1 hour 30 minutes - plus time for preparing the dough

Calories: 868 per slice

 Sangiovese sardo (Sardinia) aged 1 year (red)

For four: *For the dough: see basic pizza dough recipe on page 28.*
For the topping: ¹/₂ pound onions - 5 tablespoons milk - 1 pound plum tomatoes - 8 anchovy fillets - 4 cloves of garlic - 2 tablespoons oregano - 12 black olives - salt and pepper.

Instructions: Brush the surface of the pizza dough with olive oil; cover with a kitchen towel and let rise for 1 hour. Chop the onions, olives, tomatoes, anchovies, and garlic. Cook the onions in 2 tablespoons of the oil and the milk for a few minutes. Preheat the oven to 400 °F. Cover the pizza dough with the tomatoes, onion mixture with salt, diced anchovies, garlic and olives, and top with the oregano pepper and Parmesan cheese. Bake for 25 minutes - until golden brown.

Small puffed strips with rosemary

  About 1 hour 10 minutes - plus time for preparing the dough

Calories per portion (2 strips): 312

 Trebbiano di Romagna (Romagna) (white)

For four: *For dough: see basic pizza dough recipe on page 28 - 4 tablespoons rosemary - ¹/₄ cup olive oil.*

Instructions: Add the rosemary to the basic dough; extrude the dough through the disc and cut lengthwise into 5" long strips. Press the strips with your fingers in different places, making them hollow and pouring in some olive oil. Allow the dough to rise at room temperature for 40 minutes. When the strips of dough have almost doubled in thickness, bake in the preheated oven (350 °F) for 15-20 minutes, until golden brown.

Pastiera

 About 2 hours and 30 minutes - plus time to soak and cook the barley

Calories per slice: 565

 Ischia bianco superiore (Campania) (white)

For four: *For the dough: 1 pound plain flour measured in the PastaMatic measuring cup - ¹/₂ cup sugar - 6 tablespoons butter - 2 egg yolks - 2 tablespoons milk - 1 teaspoon baking powder - ¹/₄ teaspoon vanilla.*
For the filling: 9 ounces barley - 2 cups milk - 2 cups ricotta cheese - 6 ounces sugar - ¹/₂ cup candied citron peel - 4 eggs and 2 egg yolks - 1 orange peel, grated - ¹/₄ teaspoon cinnamon - salt.
For the baking pan: 3 tablespoons butter - 3 tablespoons plain flour.

Instructions: Soak the barley for 12 hours and cook for 1 hour in boiling water (if you use a CombiVapor it cooks in half the time). Drain the barley and cook with the milk, half of the sugar, orange peel, cinnamon and salt - simmering over low heat, stirring frequently, until all the milk is absorbed.
Remove from the heat and allow to cool. Add the ricotta cheese, candied citron peel, and 6 egg yolks. Beat the egg whites until stiff and add them to the mixture, fold through.
To prepare the dough: use the PastaMatic measuring cup. Pour the flour, sugar, butter, baking powder vanilla and salt into the PastaMatic bowl, turn on the machine, add egg yolks and milk through the opening in the lid. After 5 minutes the dough is ready. Remove the slide and extrude some dough, put back in the bowl; turn off the PastaMatic and fasten the disc for pizza (which may be preheated in hot water). Extrude the dough and cut it lengthwise as

needed to cover the bottom and sides of the baking pan (10" greased with butter and sprinkled with flour). Press borders of the strips of dough to stick together and set aside some dough. Pour in the filling and use the rest of the dough to make some 1", which you will live over the filling in a net-like manner to decorate the top of the pie. Bake in preheated oven - 350 °F - four 1 hour - cool before serving.

Small flat loaves with sage

  About 1 hour 10 minutes - plus time for preparing the dough

Calories per portion: 312

 Frascati di Fontana candida (Latium) (white)

For four: *See basic pizza dough recipe on page 28 - 5 tablespoons sage leaves - ¹/₄ cup olive oil.*

Instructions: Add the chopped sage leaves to the basic dough recipe. Extrude the dough through the disc and cut it lengthwise into 5" pieces. Press the strips of dough with your fingers in different places, making them hollow and pour in a few drops of olive oil. Allow the dough to rise at room temperature for 40 minutes. When the thickness of the strips of dough has doubled, bake for 15 minutes - at 350 °F - until golden brown.

Macaroon and chocolate cake

 About 40 minutes - plus time for preparing the dough

Calories per slice: 645

Moscato dell'Oltrepò Pavese (Lombardy) (white)

For four: *For the dough: 1 pound plain flour measured in the measuring cup - 1 teaspoon of baking powder - 2 tablespoons of bitter cocoa - 1 cup sugar - 5 ounces of butter - ¹/₄ teaspoon vanilla - pinch of salt - 3 egg yolks - 1 cup milk (which is equivalent to the measuring cup - up to the egg level for 1 pound of flour) - dash of cinnamon powder. For greasing the baking pan: 3 tablespoons butter - 4 tablespoons flour. For the filling: 20 macaroon cookies - ¹/₄ cup rum - ¹/₂ cup milk - 1 medium size orange (grate the orange peel).*

Instructions: Soak the macaroons in the rum and milk. Pour the flour, cocoa, sugar, butter, vanilla, baking powder, cinnamon and salt into the bowl. Turn the machine on; after 2 minutes add the eggs and the milk. Allow the dough to knead for 5 minutes; turn the PastaMatic off and allow the dough to sit for 1 hour and 30 minutes. Remove the slide, extrude some dough (which you will pour back into the bowl), and turn the PastaMatic off. Fasten the disc for pizza. Cut the dough lengthwise into strips that you will use to line the bottom of the baking pan (8-12" - greased with butter and dusted with flour). Keep some dough in the bowl. Line the cookies neatly over the layer of dough, sprinkle with orange peel. Fasten the disc for bread sticks and extrude the rest of the dough. Cut it lengthwise into long pieces to cover the top of the cookies. Make a net-like weave with the dough strips over the macaroons. Bake at 350 °F for 1 hour.

Quiche Lorraine

 About 1 hour 15 minutes

Calories per slice: 780

 Nebbiolo d'Alba (Piedmont) (red)

For four: *For the dough: 1 pound plain flour, measured in the PastaMatic measuring cup - 1 teaspoon salt - 2 egg yolks - 1 cup milk (equivalent to the PastaMatic measuring cup level for eggs for 1 pound of flour).*
For the filling: 7 slices of bacon - 2 eggs - $\frac{1}{2}$ cup cream - 2 tablespoons grated Parmesan cheese - pinch of nutmeg - salt and pepper to taste.
For the baking pan: 3 tablespoons of butter - 3 tablespoons of flour.

Instructions: Using the PastaMatic measuring cup, pour the flour and salt into the PastaMatic bowl. Add the softened butter (cut into small pieces) and turn the PastaMatic on. Allow the ingredients to mix properly; after a few minutes, add the egg yolks and milk through the opening of the lid (using the PastaMatic measuring cup). Knead for 5 minutes and remove slide; extrude some dough (which you will put back into the bowl). Turn the PastaMatic off and fasten the disc after having heated it with hot water. Lay the strips of dough out and cut as long as needed to fit the sides and length of your baking pan (8-12") - grease the pan with butter and dust with flour, then remove the excess flour. Arrange the strips of dough so that they cover the bottom as well as the sides of the pan and lay the slices of bacon on the bottom. Beat the eggs with the cream, grated cheese, nutmeg and salt - pour over the bacon slices. Bake for 45 minutes at 350 °F - serve hot or cold.
Variation: $\frac{1}{2}$ cup of shredded Swiss cheese

- $\frac{1}{2}$ cup chopped onion that has been sauteed in butter with $\frac{1}{2}$ cup fresh diced spinach, or mushrooms. Proceed as instructed above.

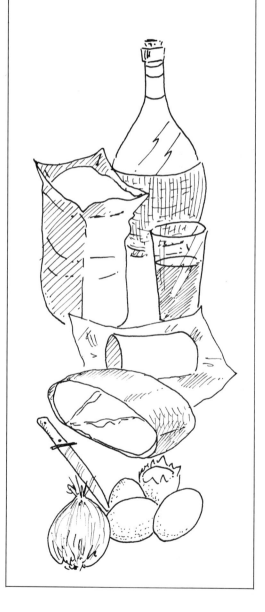

Ricotta Pie

  About 1 hour 20 minutes

Calories per portion: 724

Frascati (Latium) (red)

For four: *For the dough: see basic pizza dough recipe on page 28.*
For the filling: 2 cups of Italian ricotta cheese - 1/2 cup milk - 1 clove garlic - 4 fresh basil leaves - 1/4 cup Italian parsley - 2 eggs - 2 tablespoons grated Parmesan cheese - 3 tablespoons olive oil - salt and pepper.

Instructions: Grease a baking dish (large pie pan) with olive oil; chop the garlic, basil and parsley; grate the cheese. Lay the strips of dough side by side - overlapping slightly and pressing the borders to make them stick together - use only half of the dough to do this. Crush the ricotta cheese with a fork - adding the milk and seasoning - also the basil, parsley, garlic, cheese and eggs - mix and blend throughly. Spread the mixture over the dough and either leave pie pan open or use strips of dough to cover the top (use a fork to make holes on the top and brush with olive oil). Bake at 350 °F for 40 minutes.

Mushroom pie

  About 2 hours - plus time for preparing the dough

Calories per portion: 455

Lago di Caldaro (Alto Adige) aged 1 year (red)

For four: *For the dough: see basic pizza dough recipe on page 28.*
For the filling: 1 pound fresh mushrooms - 2 cloves of garlic - 3 tablespoons Italian parsley, chopped - olive oil - salt - 2 tablespoons butter.

Instructions: Chop the mushrooms, garlic and parsley. Lay the strips of dough side-by-side, overlapping slightly and pressing with your fingers on the borders to make them stick together (use half of the dough to do this, saving the rest for the top). Saute the mushrooms, garlic, and parsley in the butter for a few minutes. Spread a small amount of olive oil over the dough; allow the dough to rise for 40 minutes. Spread the mushroom topping over the dough; either cover the top with the rest of the dough or leave open. Bake at 350 °F for 15 minutes. You can also add cheese to the top as a variation.

Short-pastry tart with marmalade

 About 1 hour

Calories: 345 per slice

 Bella Bita Rose (Sicily) (rosé)

For six: *½ pound plain flour measured in the PastaMatic measuring cup - ½ cup sugar - 4 tablespoons butter - 1 grated lemon peel - 2 egg yolks - 1 cup marmalade - pinch of salt - 3 tablespoons milk.*

Instructions: Pour the flour, sugar, salt, lemon peel and butter into the PastaMatic bowl and begin kneading. After 1 minute add the eggs and milk and let it knead until the ingredients are mixed well. Remove the slide and extrude some dough (which you will put back into the bowl). Turn off the PastaMatic and fasten the disc for pizza (which must be preheated using hot water first). Extrude the strips of dough and lay the strips side-by-side in a baking pan (10"), pressing on the borders to make them stick together perfectly. Cover the pan with aluminium foil, press tightly on the sides for a tight fit. Bake for 30 minutes at 350 °F. Fifteen minutes before they are done, remove the aluminium foil and put the pan back in the oven. Remove the cooked dough from the baking pan and let cool; stuff with your favorite marmalade filling; marmalade can be spread over the top instead of using as a filling.

Fruit tart

 About 1 hour 30 minutes

Calories: 376 per slice

 Moscato d'Asti Spumante (Piedmont) (white)

For six: *Use the "short pastry tart" recipe on page 106, but instead of the marmalade use: 2 dozen fresh strawberries or 6 fresh peaches or 10 apricots or 3 fresh bananas or pineapple (can be canned if drained). Arrange mixed fruits for variations. Jelly - Maraschino liqueur.*
For the cream: 3 egg yolks - ½ cup sugar - 1 ounce potato flour - dash of vanilla - 1 cup milk.

Instructions: Prepare the tart (see tart marmalade recipe on page 106). While the dough is baking prepare the cream by beating the egg yolks with the sugar and the potato flour with a dash of vanilla and gradually adding the lukewarm milk. Cook the cream slowly over a low flame, stirring constantly, until the cream thickens; allow to cool, stirring occasionally to prevent the cream from forming a thin film. When the tart is baked and cool, remove from the baking pan and spread the tart with the cream and then the washed and diced fruit; then brush the top of the fruit with either thin jelly or Maraschino liqueur.

Bread

For the bread dough see page 29.

Instructions: This is the only case when you have to work manually to shape the bread, because the PastaMatic is designed to do everything else for you.
To obtain the different shapes, watch the following drawings.

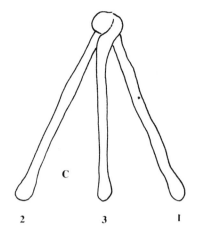

"TRECCIA" (BRAID)

The various working steps

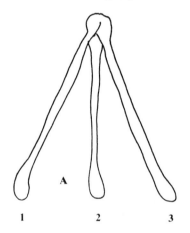

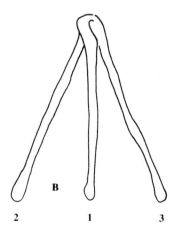

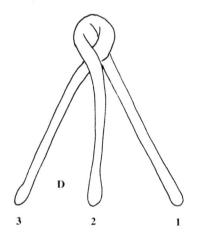

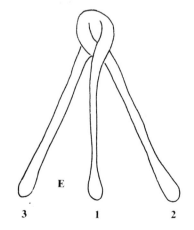

108

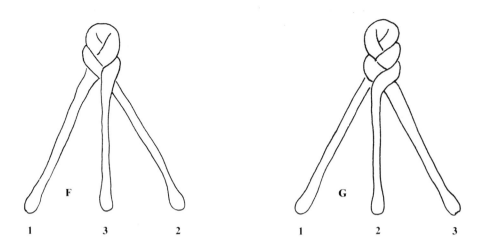

Pat the ends firmly to complete the braid

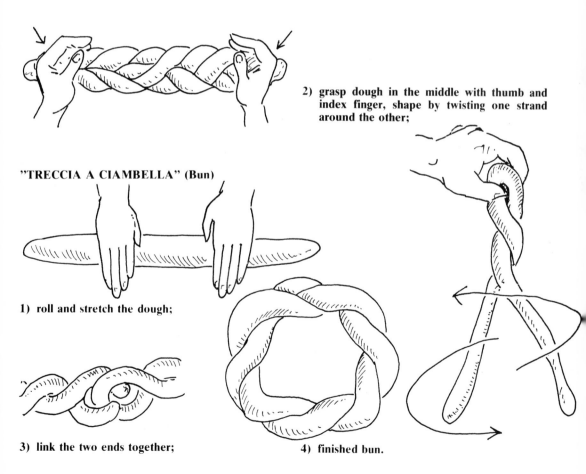

2) grasp dough in the middle with thumb and index finger, shape by twisting one strand around the other;

"TRECCIA A CIAMBELLA" (Bun)

1) roll and stretch the dough;

3) link the two ends together;

4) finished bun.

"TARTINA" (ROLL)

"ALBERO" (TREE)

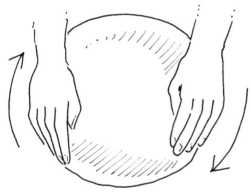

round out with the palm of the hand

cut the long shaped bread with a knife on an angle as shown

" PUGLIESE" (APULIA'S STYLE BREAD)

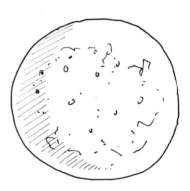

1) round out dough;

2) finished Apulia-bread.

"FRANCESONE" (LARGE FRENCH BAGUETTE STYLE BREAD)

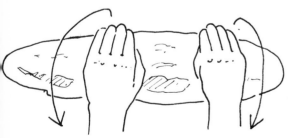

1) press down on the center, grasp the dough and pull towards you;

2) to obtain a "break" in the center of the loaf, pull each side of dough towards the center.

"CREMONESE" (CREMONA STYLE BREAD)

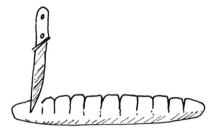

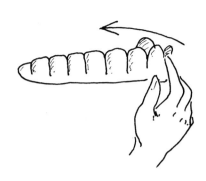

1) make short cuts on one side only;

2) round it out and press ends together;

3) finished Cremona-bread.

"FOGLIA" (LEAF)

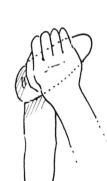

2) roll it up in a criss-cross manner;

1) with the palm tap the dough down moving in a backward motion;

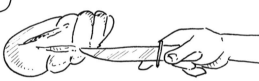

3) make two cuts with a knife on the top.

"FRANCESINO" (SMALL FRENCH STYLE BREAD)

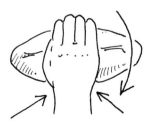

1) push and press dough in a forward motion;

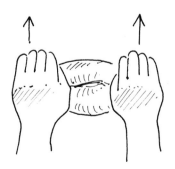

2) flatten down the two ends and push forward.

113

"PARIGINA" (PARISIAN STYLE BREAD)

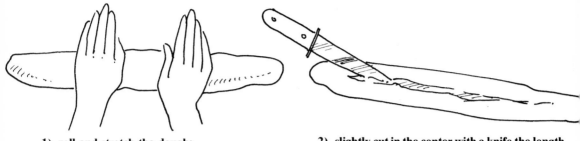

1) roll and stretch the dough;

2) slightly cut in the center with a knife the length of the loaf.

" PASTA DURA" (DURUM BREAD STYLE)

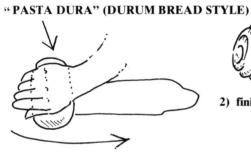

2) finished durum bread;

1) tap down with the palm moving in a backward motion;

3) this shape if allowed to leaven and slightly cut in the center, is the "Piacentino" (Piacenza style bread).

"MAGGIOLINO" STYLE BREAD

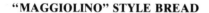

1) roll out in the same way as the Foglia style bread, but rolling the dough straight and not criss-crossed;

2) shape it;

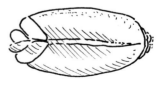

3) cut it in the center with the hand

4) finished Maggiolino bread.

114

"CIAMBELLONE"
(LARGE DOUGHNUT STYLE BREAD)

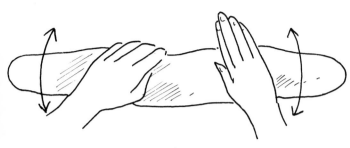

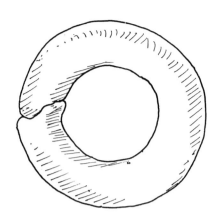

1) round out and stretch the dough;

2) press the two ends together.

"PIUMA" (PLUME STYLE BREAD)

1) stretch the dough;

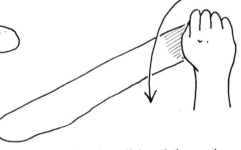

2) roll up crosswise in a slight twisting motion;

3) finished Piuma bread.

"CIABATTA" (SLIPPER STYLE BREAD)

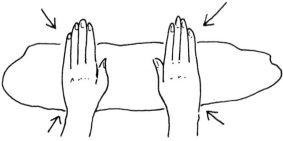

1) stretch and flatten the dough;

2) finished Ciabatta bread sprinkled with flour.

115

"FERRARESE" (FERRARA STYLE BREAD)

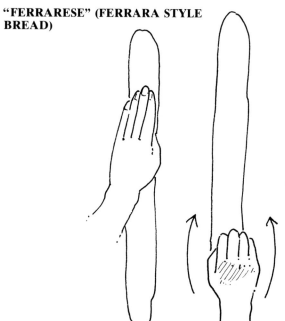

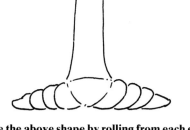

1) sprinkle dough with flour; 2) flatten and roll out;

3) make the above shape by rolling from each end towards the center, pressing the dough outwards slightly;

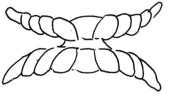

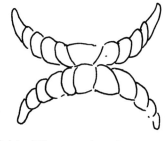

4) curl the ends as shown;

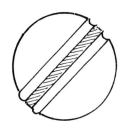

6) finished Ferrarese bread.

5) turn one section on top of the other, creating horn shape;

STENCIL TO SHAPE MANUALLY

for roll

for Modena style bread

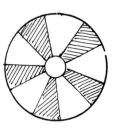

Cumin bread

Ingredients: (See basic dough for bread recipe on page 29) - 1 tablespoon cumin seeds.

Instructions: See instructions for bread, adding the cumin seeds.

Sweet corn meal bread

 About 50 minutes

Calories per portion: 346

Ingredients: 1/2 pound plain flour measured in the PastaMatic cup - 1 cup fine corn meal - 1/2 cup sugar - 6 tablespoons butter - dash of vanilla - 1 teaspoon baking powder - salt - milk (use the PastaMatic water-egg measuring cup and fill to the water level for 1 pound of flour).
For the pan: 3 tablespoons butter - 3 tablespoons flour - 3 tablespoons powder sugar.

Instructions: Pour the flour, sugar, salt, vanilla, and baking powder into the PastaMatic bowl; add the butter (which has been cut into small pieces) and knead until all the ingredients are blended.
Remove the slide and extrude some dough, then put it back into the bowl. Fasten the disc for pizza (which has been preheated with hot water) and extrude the dough. Cut the dough lengthwise into 13" long strips, cutting the strips into round pieces with the fluted pastry wheel.
Layer the strips on the baking dish (that has been greased with butter then sprinkled with plain flour). Sprinkle the strips with the powder sugar and bake at 350 °F for 15-20 minutes. (It is best to place a bowl of hot water in the oven to keep the necessary moisture in the oven).

Biscotti (cookies)

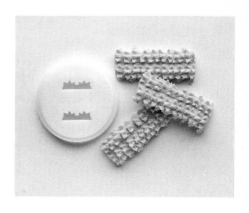

Almond cookies

 About 45 minutes

Calories per portion: 525 (for 4 cookies)

For four: *1/2 pound of plain flour measured in the measuring cup - 1/2 cup sugar - 1/2 cup slivered almonds - 1 teaspoon baking powder - 4 tablespoons butter - 1 grated lemon peel - 2 eggs - 1 tablespoon Maraschino liqueur - 3 tablespoons powder sugar - dash of salt. For the baking pan: 3 tablespoons butter, 3 tablespoons flour.*

Instructions: Pour the flour, salt, baking powder, and finely slivered almonds, with the butter and grated lemon peel into the bowl. Knead for 2 minutes to allow the ingredients to blend, then pour in the eggs and liqueur through the lid, using the measuring cup. Knead for 5-6 minutes; then remove the slide and extrude some dough (which you will put back into the bowl). Fasten the disc and cut the cookies lengthwise into 3" long pieces. Grease the baking dish with butter then sprinkle with powder sugar. Bake for 15 minutes in an oven preheated to 350 ° F.

Chestnut cookies

About 45 minutes

Calories per portion: 520 (for 4 cookies)

For four: *1/2 pound of chestnut flour measured in the PastaMatic measuring cup - 1/2 pound plain flour - 1 teaspoon baking powder - 5 ounces sugar - dash of vanilla - 4 tablespoons butter - 1 egg - salt.*

Instructions: Pour the chestnut and plain flours into the PastaMatic with the baking powder, sugar and mashed butter; knead for 1 minute. Add the eggs through the opening in the lid using the PastaMatic measuring cup and knead for 5 minutes, until all of the ingredients are blended. Remove the slide and extrude some dough (which you will put back into the bowl). Turn on the PastaMatic and fasten the disc for cookies. Cut the dough lengthwise into 3" pieces. Grease the baking pan and sprinkle with flour. Place the cookies in the dish and bake for 15 minutes at 350 °F; but do not allow to get too brown. Cool and remove to serving plate.

Coffee cookies

  About 45 minutes

Calories per portion: 525 (for 4 cookies)

For four: *¹/₂ pound plain flour measured in the PastaMatic measuring cup - 5 ounces sugar - 1 egg - 3 tablespoons butter - 1 teaspoon baking powder - dash of vanilla - salt - 2 tablespoons instant coffee - 5 tablespoons milk.*

Instructions: Pour the flour, baking powder, sugar, salt and softened butter into the PastaMatic bowl and knead for 1 minute. Add the lukewarm milk with the instant coffee using the PastaMatic measuring cup and mix well. Add the eggs and knead for 5 minutes. Remove the slide and extrude some dough; turn the machine off and fasten the disc for cookies. Cut the dough lengthwise into 2-3" long pieces and place them in the baking dish (which has been greased with butter and sprinkled with flour). Bake for 15 minutes at 350 °F, do not allow cookies to get too brown.

Wholewheat cookies

  About 40 minutes

Calories per portion: 495 (for 4 cookies)

For four: *¹/₂ pound wholewheat flour measured in the PastaMatic measuring cup - ¹/₃ cup plain flour - ¹/₂ cup sugar - 3 tablespoons butter - 2 eggs - 1 grated lemon peel - dash of vanilla - 1 teaspoon baking powder - salt.*

Instructions: Pour the wholewheat flour, plain flour and baking powder with the sugar, salt, lemon peel and softened butter into the PastaMatic bowl and knead for 1 minute. Add the eggs through the opening in the lid using the PastaMatic measuring cup and knead for 5 minutes, until all of the ingredients are blended. Remove the slide and extrude some dough (which you will put back into the bowl) and turn off the PastaMatic. Fasten the disc for cookies and cut the dough lengthwise into 3" long pieces. Grease and dust the baking pan with flour, then line the cookies in the oven dish and bake for 15 minutes at 350 °F.

Spicy cookies

 About 45 minutes

Calories per portion: 527 (for 4 cookies)

For six: *½ pound wholewheat flour measured in the PastaMatic measuring cup - ½ pound plain flour measured in the Pasta-Matic measuring cup - 1 egg - 5 ounces sugar - dash of vanilla - 1 teaspoon baking powder - 3 tablespoons butter - 2 tablespoons honey - 3 tablespoons milk - dash cinnamon powder - 2 teaspoons ground ginger powder - salt.*
For baking dish: butter and flour.

Instructions: Pour the flour, salt, baking powder, butter, honey, cinnamon powder, and ginger into the PastaMatic bowl and knead. After a couple of minutes add the eggs and milk using the PastaMatic measuring cup. Knead for 5 minutes, then remove the slide and extrude some dough (which you will put back into the bowl). Turn the PastaMatic off and fasten the disc for cookies. Cut the dough lengthwise into 3" pieces. Line the cookies in the baking pan (which has been greased with butter and sprinkled with flour). Bake at 350 °F for 15 minutes.

Parmesan cheese snacks

 About 40 minutes

Calories per portion: 637 (for 4 cookies)

For four: *½ pound plain flour measured in the PastaMatic measuring cup - 3 ounces grated Parmesan cheese - 2 eggs - 3 ounces butter - pinch of salt - 1 egg white.*

Instructions: Grease the baking pan with butter and sprinkle with flour.
Pour the flour, salt, cheese and butter into the PastaMatic bowl and knead; after 1 minute add the eggs through the opening of the lid using the PastaMatic cup; knead for 3-4 minutes, until all ingredients are mixed. Remove the slide and extrude some dough (which you will put back into the bowl).
Turn off the PastaMatic and fasten the disc for cookies. Cut the dough lengthwise into 2" pieces. Line them in the baking dish and brush with slightly beaten egg white. Bake at 300 °F for 20 minutes; serve hot or cold with cocktails.

Grissini
(bread sticks)

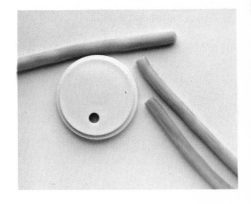

Bread sticks (basic dough)

 About 1 hour

Calories per portion: 325 (for 6 bread sticks)

For four: *1 pound all-purpose flour measured in the measuring cup - 2 tablespoons olive oil - 1 package (¹/₄ oz dry active yeast) - 1 large egg - 1 teaspoon salt - 1 tablespoon sugar - warm water to the egg level for ¹/₂ pound flour in the measuring cup.*

Instructions: Add the sugar and yeast to the water and let rest for 10 minutes. Place the flour and salt in the bowl and lock the cover in place. Run the machine for 30 seconds; with the machine still running slowly add the egg; run the machine for 2 more minutes. Slowly pour in the dissolved yeast mixture. Drop the oil in slowly and run for 2 minutes (should be the same consistency as pasta). Let the dough rest in the covered bowl for 1¹/₂ hours. Remove the dough and squeeze out the air - tear into walnut-size pieces and return to bowl. Oil three baking sheets. Fit the machine with the disc and extrude the dough, cutting into 6 or 12" long pieces. Place on the sheets, space them and turn to coat in the oil. Let them rise for 1 hour. Heat the oven to 400 °F. Bake for 15-20 minutes.

Wholewheat bread sticks

 About 1 hour 15 minutes

Calories per portion: 319 (for 4 bread sticks)

For four: *¹/₂ pound whole wheat flour measured in the PastaMatic cup - ¹/₂ pound all-purpose flour measured in the Pasta-Matic cup - 3 tablespoons olive oil - 1 package (¹/₄ ounce) dry active yeast - 1 teaspoon salt - 1 tablespoon sugar - 1 large egg - warm water to the egg level (on the PastaMatic cup) for ¹/₂ pound flour.*

Instructions: Follow the recipe for the bread sticks on page 122, using the wholewheat flour and all-purpose flour together and increasing the olive oil to 3 tablespoons.

Bread sticks and tarallucci

Orecchiette with turnip-tops

Orecchiette with turnip-tops

 About 1 hour 15 minutes

Calories per portion: 745 (for 3 ounces)

 Castellana Grotte rosato (Apulia) (rosé)

For four: *For the dough:* $^1/_2$ *pound all-purpose flour measured in the PastaMatic cup -* $^1/_2$ *pound durum wheat flour measured in the PastaMatic cup - 1 egg - water measured in the PastaMatic measuring cup to the water level for 1 pound of flour - remove 1 tablespoon of flour - salt.*
For the sauce: 1 pound turnip-tops - $^1/_4$ *cup olive oil - 1 clove garlic - 4 flat anchovy fillets.*

Instructions: Pour the flour and salt into the PastaMatic bowl and knead; pour the water and eggs in slowly, using the PastaMatic cup. When all the ingredients are perfectly mixed, remove the slide and extrude some dough. Turn off the machine and fasten the disc for bread sticks; extrude the dough and lay on the kitchen board, sprinkle with flour. Cut dough lengthwise into 3" long pieces and press each piece of dough with your finger in a sliding movement to obtain the "orecchiette shape"; set aside and prepare the turnip-tops. Use only the tender parts and the tops; discard the yellow ones and use the green. Wash and cook in salted boiling water until tender; drain and keep hot. Use the same water to cook the orecchiette, under cook it by 2 minutes; drain the pasta and add to a large frying pan with the turnip-tops and add the crushed garlic and mashed anchovies, that have been pre-cooked with the oil. Stir through and mix the ingredients well, and cook for 4-5 minutes. Serve hot.

Tarallucci

 About 50 minutes

Calories per portion: 440

 Regaleali rosso (Sicily) (red)

For eight: *1 pound plain flour measured in the PastaMatic cup -* $^1/_4$ *cup olive oil -* $^1/_2$ *cup sugar - 2 tablespoons milk - 4 tablespoon Marsala wine - salt. Grease the baking dish with butter and dust with plain flour.*

Instructions: Pour the flour, sugar, and salt into the PastaMatic bowl. Knead for 1 minute. Add the oil, milk and Marsala wine slowly, using your liquid measuring cup if desired. Knead for 4 minutes. Remove the slide and extrude some dough. Turn off the machine and fasten the disc for bread sticks. Extrude the dough and cut lengthwise into 5" long pieces. Press the two ends of each piece of dough and stick them together, into a ring form. Lay the tarallucci in the baking dish, spacing properly, and bake at 350 °F for 20 minutes.

Chioccioline with chocolate

 About 40 minutes

Calories per portion: 517

For six: 1 pound all-porpose flour measured in the PastaMatic measuring cup - 2 tablespoons bitter cocoa - ¹/₂ cup sugar - 1 grated orange peel - 3 egg yolks - milk (enough to fill the measuring cup up to the egg level for 1 pound of flour) - dash of cinnamon powder, 2 tablespoons butter. Grease the baking dish with butter and dust with flour.

Instructions: Pour the flour, cocoa, sugar, orange peel, softened butter, cinnamon powder and salt into the PastaMatic bowl and knead. After a few minutes add the milk and eggs using the PastaMatic cup. Knead for 5 minutes more, then remove the slide and extrude some dough. Turn off the PastaMatic and fasten the disc for bread sticks. Extrude the dough and cut lengthwise into 8" long pieces. Roll the strips of dough around one of their ends into a "coil-like shape". Lay the Chioccioline evenly - spacing properly - in a pre-greased baking dish and bake at 400 °F for 15 minutes.

Pisarei with beans

 About 1 hour 40 minutes

Calories per portion: 761

 Lambrusco Grasparossa di Castel-vetro (Emilia) (red)

For four: For the dough: 1 pound plain flour measured in the PastaMatic cup - ¹/₃ cup fine breadcrumbs - water (enough to reach the egg level for 1 pound of flour in the PastaMatic measuring cup) salt - Parmesan cheese.
For the sauce: 1 cup boiled red kidney beans - 3 tablespoons butter - ¹/₄ pound pancetta or ham - 3 tablespoons olive oil - 1 medium onion - 1 carrot - 2 stalks celery - 7 fresh basil leaves - ¹/₄ cup chopped Italian parsley - 1 clove garlic - 1 cup tomato puree - salt and pepper.

Instructions: For the dough: pour the flour, breadcrumbs and salt into the PastaMatic bowl and knead; after 1 minute add the cold water (using the PastaMatic cup) and knead for 4 minutes. Remove the slide and extrude some dough. Turn the machine off and fasten the disc for bread sticks; cut the dough lengthwise into 1" long pieces. Press each piece of dough with your finger in a sliding movement and make them hollow (pisarei are the typical gnocchi shape of Piacenza). Cook the pisarei and drain; toss with Parmesan cheese.
For the sauce: chop the ham; dice the vegetables, parsley, basil, onions and garlic. Saute in the oil for 5-8 minutes; add the pre-boiled beans and blend through. Add the tomato puree and salt and pepper; allow to cook for 30 minutes. Add the pisarei and blend through, serve with more grated Parmesan cheese.

Gnocchi

***Basic dough: With potatoes (or Spinach Gnocchi
- made with spinach)***
Cooking time: 2-3 minutes
To be used: Drained with various sauces (3-4 ounces
per portion)

Gnocchi with cheese

   About 20 minutes - plus time for
preparing the gnocchi

Calories per portion: 584

 Barbera d'Asti (Piedmont) aged 1
year (red)

For four: *For the gnocchi see basic dough
recipe on page 27.*
*For the sauce: ¹/₂ pound Italian fontina
cheese - 4 tablespoons grated Parmesan
cheese - 3 tablespoons butter - 1 clove of
garlic - salt.*

Instructions: Crush the garlic and cook for
a few minutes with the butter. Prepare the
gnocchi as instructed on page 27. Cook
and drain, then transfer to a heated serving bowl. Dice the fontina cheese and
toss through with the Parmesan cheese
and add butter-garlic sauce. Blend
through the gnocchi and serve immediately.

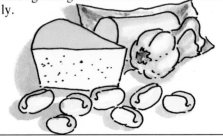

Gnocchi with four cheeses

  About 15 minutes - plus time for
preparing the gnocchi

Calories per portion: 482

Castel Chiuro della Valtellina
(Lombardy) (red)

For four: *For the gnocchi see basic dough
recipe on page 27.*
*For the sauce: ¹/₄ cup diced Italian fontina
cheese - ¹/₂ cup mozzarella cheese - ¹/₄ cup
Swiss cheese - 2 tablespoons butter - 2 tablespoons grated Parmesan cheese pepper.*

Instructions: Prepare the gnocchi as instructed on page 27.
Cut the cheese into small cubes. Boil the
water and cook the gnocchi, then drain
and transfer into a heated serving bowl
and toss with the four cheeses and melted
butter. Sprinkle with fresh ground pepper
and add more Parmesan cheese, toss and
blend, serve immediately.

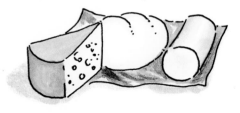

Gnocchi with four cheeses

Gnocchi with curry powder

 About 40 minutes - plus time for preparing the gnocchi

Calories per portion: 456

 Rosé di Bolgheri (Tuscany) (rosé)

For four: *For the gnocchi see basic dough recipe on page 27.*
For the sauce: 1 small onion - ¹/₄ cup olive oil - 2 tablespoons butter - ¹/₂ pound fresh, diced plum tomatoes (or 1 cup tomato sauce) - ¹/₂ cup milk - 1 teaspoon curry powder - grated Parmesan cheese - salt and pepper.

Instructions: Prepare the gnocchi as instructed on page 27. Saute the chopped onion in the butter for a few minutes. Add the diced tomatoes (or sauce), the milk, salt and pepper and cook for 8-10 minutes.
Add the curry powder and cook 5 minutes, stirring constantly. Cook and drain the gnocchi and sprinkle with Parmesan cheese. Toss thoroughly. Add the sauce and blend again thoroughly. Serve immediately.

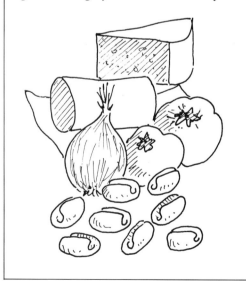

Gnocchi with gorgonzola cheese

 About 15 minutes - plus time for preparing the gnocchi

Calories per portion: 524

 Sassella Valtellina Superiore (Lombardy) (red)

For four: *For the gnocchi see basic dough recipe on page 27.*
For the sauce: ¹/₃ cup cream - 3 tablespoons butter - ¹/₂ pound Italian gorgonzola cheese - grated Parmesan cheese - pepper.

Instructions: Cook the gnocchi and drain. Transfer to a warmed serving bowl. Crumble and melt the gorgonzola cheese, stirring with a wooden spoon and add the cream and butter and heat over a low flame, stirring to a smooth texture.
Sprinkle the gnocchi with the pepper and Parmesan cheese and then toss with the cheese sauce until evenly coated.

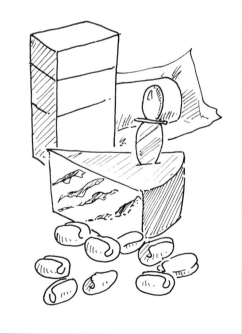

Stuffed cheese snacks

 About 50 minutes

Calories per portion: 371 (four pieces)

For six: *¹/₂ pound plain flour measured in the PastaMatic measuring cup - 3 tablespoons Parmesan cheese - 3 tablespoons butter - 1 egg and 1 egg yolk - 4 tablespoons milk - 1 teaspoon baking powder - 1 grated lemon peel (yellow portion only) - salt.*
For stuffing: ¹/₂ cup grated Parmesan cheese - 2 tablespoons cream - 2 drops Tabasco sauce.
Butter and plain flour for baking sheet.

Instructions: Pour the flour, grated cheese, baking powder, grated lemon peel and butter into the PastaMatic bowl. After kneading for a few minutes, pour in the eggs and milk using the PastaMatic cup and knead for 5 minutes. Remove the slide and extrude some dough. Turn off the PastaMatic and fasten the disc for gnocchi into place. Cut the dough into 3" long pieces. Mix the grated cheese, the cream and the Tabasco sauce. Use this sauce to fill the hollow pieces of dough. Line the stuffed pieces of dough on a baking sheet that has been greased with butter, and sprinkled with flour. (Make sure the stuffing side faces upwards). Bake in a hot oven (preheated at 400°F) for 15 minutes. Serve hot or cold with cocktails.

Rigatini with gin sauce

 About 45 minutes

Calories per portion: 366 (four pieces)

For six: *¹/₂ pound plain flour measured in the PastaMatic measuring cup - 3 ounces sugar - 4 tablespoons butter - 3 tablespoons gin (liqueur) - 2 tablespoons milk - dash of vanilla - 1 teaspoon baking powder - 1 grated lemon peel (yellow portion only) - salt.*
For the baking pan: butter and plain flour.

Instructions: Pour the flour, sugar, baking powder, butter, grated lemon peel and salt into the PastaMatic bowl and knead for 2 minutes. Add the gin and milk through the opening of the lid and knead for 5 minutes. Remove the slide. Extrude some dough and turn off the PastaMatic and fasten the disc on for gnocchi. Cut the dough lengthwise into 3" long pieces and line them evenly on a baking sheet (greased with butter and then sprinkled with flour). Keep the fluted side facing upwards and press rigatini gently. Bake in a hot oven for 15 minutes at 400°F.

Conchigliette rigate
(small shells)

Also called Sardinian - small Gnocchi or Malloreddus

Recommended kind of dough: With eggs - with whole-wheat flour - with durum wheat flour

Cooking time: 8 minutes - 6 minutes - 10 minutes

To be used: Drained (4 ounces per portion) - for soups (1 ounce per portion)

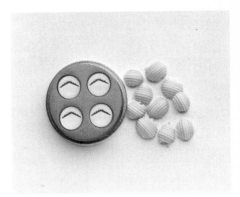

Peppers stuffed with conchigliette

  About 1 hour 30 minutes

Calories per portion: 467

  Five Roses (Apulia) (rosé)

For four: *¹/₂ pound conchigliette rigate - 4 peppers - 10 basil leaves - 1 clove garlic - 1 tablespoon capers - 4 flat anchovy fillets - 1 cup diced mozzarella cheese - 4 plum tomatoes - 1 tablespoon chopped chives - 2 shallot onions - 2 tablespoons olive oil (plus enough olive oil to grease the pan) - salt and pepper.*

Instructions: Wash and dry the peppers and cut into halves; dice the garlic, onions, anchovies, tomatoes, cheese, and basil leaves. Cook and drain the pasta (cook for only 3 minutes) then transfer to a heated mixing bowl. Toss with the chopped basil leaves, capers, garlic, anchovies and chives. Mix in the tomatoes, mozzarella cheese, oil, salt and pepper - blend thoroughly. Stuff the peppers with this mixture and line in a baking pan (which has been greased with oil). Bake at 350 °F for 45 minutes.

Malloreddus with Sardinian ragu sauce

  About 1 hour 10 minutes

Calories per portion: 873

  Sant'Antioco (Sardinia) (red)

For four: *1 pound conchigliette rigate - ¹/₂ pound pork meat (ground) - ¹/₄ pound ground lamb meat - 3 tablespoons lard - 1 cup tomato puree - 1 medium onion - 3 tablespoons chopped Italian parsley - 8 fresh basil leaves - 6 sage leaves (or ¹/₄ teaspoon dried sage) - 3 tablespoons olive oil - Romano cheese - salt and pepper.*

Instructions: Dice the onion, parsley, basil and sage leaves. Saute the onion in the lard for a few minutes, add the pork and lamb meat and cook for 10 minutes. Add the tomato puree, salt and pepper and cook for 45 minutes over low heat thinning the sauce with some lukewarm water. Cook the pasta and drain; toss with Romano cheese; pour sauce over the pasta and toss through. Serve immediately.

130

Peppers stuffed with conchigliette

Malloreddus with Sardinian ragu sauce

Chick pea and pasta soup

 About 30 minutes - plus time to soak and cook the chick peas

Calories per portion: 674

Cerasuolo d'Abruzzo (rosé)

For four: *¹/₂ pound conchigliette rigate - 2 cups fresh chick peas or canned, drained - 3 flat anchovy fillets - 1 clove of garlic - ¹/₂ teaspoon Italian herb seasoning - 1 medium onion - 4 tablespoons olive oil - 1 cup milk - 1 stock cube (vegetable or chicken) - grated Parmesan cheese - salt and pepper.*

Instructions: Soak the chick peas in lukewarm water for about 8 hours (canned variety can be used immediately). Drain and cook the fresh chick peas for 1 hour in about 9 cups of water (if you use the Combi-Vapor pot it takes only 40 minutes); cook canned chick peas for 10 minutes. Dice the onion, garlic, and herb seasoning, then saute in the oil for a few minutes, add the crushed anchovies and allow to cook for 5 minutes, stirring often. Add the milk to the chick peas and the cooking water - add the stock cube and the onion mixture and bring to a boil. Add the pasta and cook until it is firm to the bite; season with salt and pepper. Cook for 5 minutes on a medium heat; then serve in warm bowls with more grated cheese on top.

Vegetable soup

 About 1 hour 10 minutes

Calories per portion: 467

Castel del Monte rosato (Apulia) (rosé)

For four: *¹/₂ pound conchigliette rigate - ¹/₂ pound fresh green beans - 1 medium onion - 2 medium zucchini - 2 stalks celery (leaves also) - 2 carrots - 2 leeks - 1 large potato - 3 plum tomatoes - 1 cup fresh or frozen peas - ¹/₂ cup white beans - 1 cup fresh spinach leaves - 2 tablespoons olive oil - 1 stock cube (vegetable or chicken) - ¹/₂ cup pesto sauce (see page 82) - 2 tablespoons grated Romano cheese - ¹/₄ cup chopped Italian parsley - salt and pepper.*

Instructions: Wash and chop the vegetables, add to a large pot filled with 10 cups of water; add the olive oil and stock cube and allow to cook over a medium heat for 40 minutes. Bring to a boil and add the pasta and cook for 3 minutes. Add the parsley, cheese salt and pepper and pesto sauce and cook for a few more minutes, stirring constantly. Serve in warmed soup bowls - sprinkle with more Romano cheese on top.

Cauliflower and pasta soup

About 30 minutes

Calories per portion: 377

Cacc'è mitte di Lucera rosato (Apulia) (rosé)

For four: *½ pound conchigliette. rigate - 1 small head of cauliflower - 1 clove garlic - 3 shallot onions - 3 tablespoons chopped parsley - 1 stock cube (vegetable or chicken) - 4 tablespoons olive oil - grated Parmesan cheese - salt and pepper.*

Instructions: Chop the cauliflower, garlic, onion, parsley, and grate the cheese. In a large pot, saute the onions and garlic in the oil over low heat for a few minutes. Add 10 cups of water, the stock cube and the cauliflower and cook for 20 minutes. Bring to a boil and cook the pasta for 3 minutes. Season with salt and pepper. Before serving, add the parsley and grated cheese.

Conchigliette soup

About 45 minutes

Calories per portion: 290

Chianti dei Colli (Tuscany) aged 1 year (red)

For four: *½ pound conchigliette rigate - 9 cups chicken broth (or use stock cubes) - 1 cup boiled and diced chicken meat - ¼ cup chopped parsley - 2 tablespoons grated Parmesan cheese - 2 egg yolks - salt and pepper.*

Instructions: Boil and dice the chicken meat; mix with parsley and grated cheese. Beat the egg yolks and mix with the chicken mixture. Bring the broth to a boil, add the pasta, salt and pepper and cook for a few minutes. Add the chicken meat mixture and stir through; cook for 5 minutes at medium heat. Serve warm, topped with grated cheese.

Pasta del contadino (farmer's pasta)

Recommended kind of dough: Wholewheat flour - durum wheat flour
Cooking time: 12 minutes - 8 minutes
To be used: Drained (4 ounces per portion). Cut the pasta lengthwise into 6" long pieces. With broth or vegetable soup (2 ounces per portion). Cut the pasta lengthwise into 1½" long pieces.

Farmer's pasta with eggplants

 About 50 minutes

Calories per portion: 572

 Sangiovese di Romagna (Emilia-Romagna) aged 1 year (red)

For four: 1 pound farmer's pasta - 1 large onion - 1 stalk celery - 1 carrot - 2 tablespoons chopped basil - 1 clove garlic - ¼ teaspoon Italian herb seasoning - 1 cup tomato puree - 2 small eggplants - 4 tablespoons olive oil - 3 tablespoons chopped parsley - salt and pepper - grated Pecorino cheese.

Instructions: Chop the carrot, celery, onion, garlic, basil and tomatoes, saute in 3 tablespoons olive oil for 15 minutes. Add the herb seasoning, salt and pepper and allow to cook for 20 minutes. Dice the eggplants and saute in olive oil, stirring often, for 10 minutes. Add the tomato sauce with the chopped parsley and cook for 8 minutes. Cook and drain the pasta, toss with the sauce; serve immediately. Grated Pecorino cheese can be added to each serving, very lightly.

Lentil and pasta soup

 About 1 hour

Calories per portion: 388

 Rossese di Dolceacqua (Liguria) aged 1 year (red)

For four: ½ pound farmer's pasta - 3 tablespoons butter - 1 medium onion - 2 tablespoons lard - 2 cloves garlic - 1 cup lentils (pre-soaked) - 1 cup tomato sauce - grated Parmesan cheese - salt and pepper - ¼ cup diced parsley - ¼ teaspoon Italian herb seasoning.

Instructions: Chop the onion, garlic, parsley and soak the lentils. Use a large pot to saute the onion and garlic in the butter for a few minutes. Add the tomato sauce, herb seasoning and lentils and cook for 10 minutes. Pour 10 cups of boiling water into the sauce and bring to a boil. Add the pasta and cook for a few minutes (pasta must be cut into long strips).
Remove from the heat; season with salt, pepper, grated cheese and the chopped parsley.

Farmer's pasta with anchovies and parsley

  About 20 minutes

Calories per portion: 568

Galestro (Tuscany) (white)

For four: 1 pound farmer's pasta (cut into 3" long pieces) - 3 cloves of garlic - ¹/₄ cup diced Italian parsley - 4 flat anchovy fillets - 2 tablespoons fine breadcrumbs - 4 tablespoons olive oil - pepper.

Instructions: Crush the garlic, chop the parsley and mash the anchovies. Saute the garlic in the oil with the anchovy pasta for a few minutes, then add the parsley and continue to cook for 4 more minutes. Turn off the heat and remove to a cool surface. Add the breadcrumbs and stir through. Cook and drain the pasta and toss with the sauce.

Pasta with zucchini soup "Amalfi style"

  About 45 minutes

Calories per portion: 378

Cerasuolo d'Abruzzo (Abruzzo) (rosé)

For four: ¹/₂ pound farmer's pasta - 4 small zucchini - 3 tablespoons butter - 2 tablespoons olive oil - 2 eggs - 4 tablespoons grated Parmesan cheese - ¹/₄ cup chopped Italian parsley - ¹/₄ teaspoon Italian herb seasoning - 3 tablespoons diced basil leaves - salt and pepper - 1 medium onion - 10 cups boiling water with 1 stock cube (vegetable or chicken).

Instructions: Wash and dice the zucchini, parsley, basil leaves and onion. In a large pan, saute the zucchini, onion and the seasoning in the butter for 8 minutes, stirring often. Slowly, pour the 10 cups of boiling water into the pan and boil for about 30 minutes. Add the pasta (cut into 1¹/₂" long pieces) and cook for a few minutes; then remove from the heat. Beat the eggs with the grated cheese, parsley and basil and add to the soup; stir through and serve immediately.

Farmer's pasta with onions

  About 1 hour

Calories per portion: 548

Rosso Conero (Marche) aged 1 year (red)

For four: 1 pound farmer's pasta - 3 medium onions - 1/4 cup olive oil - 1 cup tomato sauce or puree from fresh plum tomatoes - 4 tablespoons milk - grated Parmesan cheese - salt and pepper - 3 tablespoons chopped parsley.

Instructions: Peel and dice the onions and parsley. Using a heavy frying pan, saute the onions in the oil and milk until golden brown. Add the tomato sauce, salt, pepper and parsley and cook for 15 minutes. Cook and drain the pasta and toss with the onion sauce then sprinkle with Parmesan cheese and toss through.

Farmer's pasta with egg-plant and pepper sauce

  About 1 hour

Calories per portion: 583

Etna bianco (Sicily) (white)

For four: 1 pound farmer's pasta - 3 small eggplants - 2 red peppers - 1 green pepper - 2 cloves of garlic - 1 medium onion - 1 cup tomato puree or tomato sauce - 1/4 cup olive oil - 6 black olives - 8 fresh basil leaves or 1/2 teaspoon Italian herb seasoning - 2 flat anchovies - 1 tablespoon capers - 1/4 cup chopped Italian parsley - grated Romano cheese - salt and pepper.

Instructions: Chop the onion, eggplants, peppers, garlic, basil leaves, anchovies and pit and chop the olives. Saute the onion, garlic, peppers, eggplants and herb seasoning in the oil, stirring often, for 8-10 minutes. Add the tomato puree, olives, capers, anchovies and half of the parsley and basil and cook for 10 minutes. Season with salt and pepper and stir through. Cook and drain the pasta and toss with the sauce and fresh herbs; sprinkle with Romano cheese.

Fili d'oro

(Golden threads)

Recommended kind of dough: With eggs
Cooking time: 1-2 minutes
To be used: Drained (4 ounces per portion) - for soups
(2 ounces per portion)
Variation: Ring-shaped cakes (use metal part of the
disc)

Fili d'oro croquettes

 About 50 minutes

Calories per portion: 619

Rosé di Bolgheri (Tuscany) (rosé)

For four: ¹/₂ pound fili d'oro - 3 table-spoons butter - 2 tablespoons Parmesan cheese - ¹/₄ pound lean ham - ¹/₂ pound mozzarella cheese - 2 eggs - 1 cup fine breadcrumbs - 2 cups vegetable oil - ¹/₄ teaspoon Italian herb seasoning - ¹/₂ cup plain flour - salt and pepper.

Instructions: Use a bowl to beat the eggs in. Pour the flour and breadcrumbs into a paper towel. Cook the pasta in salted, boiling water and drain after 1 minute; toss with the Parmesan and butter, then set aside to cool. Take a strip of pasta and lay a small piece of ham and mozzarella with some herb seasoning in the middle and press the pasta in your hands in a "croquette form". Roll the croquettes in the flour, then dip in the eggs and roll in the breadcrumbs. Heat the vegetable oil in a large deep pan; when very hot, carefully drop the croquettes into the oil and fry. Drain and lie on paper towels to remove excess oil. Serve hot with a tomato or cheese sauce.

Fili d'oro with caviar

 About 15 minutes

Calories per portion: 468

Trentino Riesling (Trentino-Alto Adige) (white)

For four: 1 pound fili d'oro - 1 small jar of caviar - 4 tablespoons cream - 2 table-spoons of butter - 1 teaspoon lemon juice - 3 tablespoons finely chopped parsley - salt.

Instructions: Cook and drain the pasta and remove after 1-2 minutes; transfer to a large, warm serving bowl. Pour cream over the pasta and toss through. Add the diced butter, caviar, parsley and lemon juice; blend through the pasta very gently. Serve immediately.

Fili d'oro croquettes

Fili d'oro with caviar

Fili d'oro "au gratin"

 About 1 hour

Calories per portion: 728

Refosco dal peduncolo rosso (Friuli) (red)

For four: 1 pound fili d'oro - 4 tablespoons butter - 1 cup cream - ¹/₄ cup grated Parmesan cheese - 3 eggs - 1 cup shredded mozzarella cheese - ¹/₄ pound lean ham - 8 basil leaves - 8 black olives - 4 tablespoons fine breadcrumbs - salt and pepper.

Instructions: Beat the eggs in a mixing bowl; soften the butter; shread the cheese; chop the ham and dice the olives. Cook and drain the pasta; immediately toss with the butter, cream, eggs and Parmesan cheese. Grease a large baking dish with the butter and sprinkle with breadcrumbs. Line the bottom of the baking dish with half of the pasta, then diced ham, mozzarella, diced basil leaves, and olives. Cover with the remaining pasta; sprinkle with breadcrumbs and small pieces of butter. Bake for 15 minutes at 350 °F, until top is golden brown. Serve immediately.

Ring-shaped cakes

If you divide the disc for fili d'oro into two parts and use the metal part only, you can get an interesting variation: use the dough extruded from the five, big holes to bake delicious ring-shaped cakes; the dough is nicely fluted. You can prepare ¹/₂ pound ring-shaped cakes in less than 15 minutes. Think how time saving the PastaMatic has made your baking and preparation of such desserts that would normally require rolling the dough by hand to prepare the cakes and the mixing.

Peasant's ring-shaped cakes

 About 30 minutes

Calories per portion: 532 (four pieces)

For six: *1 pound plain flour measured in the PastaMatic measuring cup - $\frac{1}{2}$ cup sugar - 1 teaspoon baking powder - $\frac{1}{4}$ teaspoon vanilla - 3 ounces butter - 2 eggs - dash of salt.*

Instructions: Pour the flour, sugar, baking powder, salt and butter (softened and cut into small pieces) into the PastaMatic bowl and knead for 3 minutes. Add the eggs (which have been slightly beaten with a fork) and knead for 5 minutes. Remove the slide and extrude some dough; turn off the PastaMatic and fasten the disc - using the metal part only (if the disc moves during extrusion, this is normal until the pasta is forced, then the disc movement disappears). Cut the dough lengthwise into 5" long pieces; overlap the two ends of each strip slightly and press together so that they adhere perfectly, forming a ring-shaped cake. Lay the rings of dough in the baking pan (which has been pre-greased with butter and sprinkled with flour) and bake at 350 °F for 15 minutes.

Two-color ring-shaped cakes

 About 15 minutes

Calories per portion: 532 (four pieces)

For six: *See ring-shaped cakes recipe on page 141. Add 1 pound plain chocolate.*

Instructions: Melt the chocolate over low heat, stirring constantly, until smooth, then cool.
Dip only one half of each ring-shaped cake into the melted chocolate and lay the cakes on a cake grill to dry. Remove gently, and transfer to a serving plate.

Maccheroni quadrati

(square maccheroni)

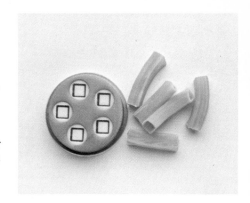

Recommended kind of dough: With eggs - with whole-wheat flour - with durum wheat flour
Cooking time: 8 minutes - 10 minutes - 7 minutes
To be used: Drained (4 ounces per portion)
Variation: Quadratini. To be used either with broth or with vegetable soup (2 ounces per portion). Cut the pasta lengthwise into ¹/₄" long pieces.

Maccheroni quadrati with tomato sauce

 About 25 minutes

Calories per portion: 523

 Torgiano rosso (Umbria) aged 1-2 years (red)

For four: 1 pound maccheroni quadrati - 2 cups tomato puree or tomato sauce - 3 tablespoons chopped parsley - ¹/₄ teaspoon Italian herb seasoning - 1 tablespoon capers - 2 cloves garlic - ¹/₄ cup olive oil - grated Parmesan cheese - salt and pepper.

Instructions: Heat the garlic in oil until golden colored, then remove. Add the tomato sauce with the parsley, capers and herb seasoning and simmer for 15 minutes. Taste for salt and pepper.
Cook and drain the pasta.
Toss with the sauce, then grated Parmesan cheese.

Maccheroni quadrati with anchovies, olives, cream

 About 30 minutes

Calories per portion: 548

 Pinot grigio dell'Alto Adige - Rülander (Trentino-Alto Adige) (white)

For four: 1 pound maccheroni quadrati - 2 cloves garlic - 4 anchovies - 1 tablespoon capers - 8 black olives - 2 tablespoons butter - ¹/₂ cup cream - dash of pepper.

Instructions: Melt the butter and saute the chopped garlic and anchovies for 4 minutes. Add the capers and olives (remove the pits and chop). Cook for 10 minutes, and add the cream and allow to thicken over low heat, stirring often.
Season with the pepper. Cook and drain the pasta. Toss with the sauce and sprinkle with more pepper.

Maccheroni quadrati with anchovies, olives, cream

Maccheroni quadrati with bacon

 About 40 minutes

Calories per portion: 803

 Bardolino (Venetia) (red)

For four: *1 pound maccheroni quadrati - 2 tablespoons butter - ¹/₂ pound bacon or pancetta - ¹/₂ cup dry white wine - ¹/₂ pound plum tomatoes - 4 tablespoons chopped parsley - grated Pecorino or Parmesan cheese - salt and pepper.*

Instructions: Dice the bacon, butter, tomatoes and parsley. Saute the bacon in the butter (add the bacon when the butter is hot and foaming and cook until crisp). Add the wine and cook for 5 minutes, stirring constantly. Add the tomatoes and cook 15 minutes longer over medium heat. Sprinkle with the parsley, salt and pepper, and stir through. Cook and drain the pasta. Toss with the grated cheese and then sauce.

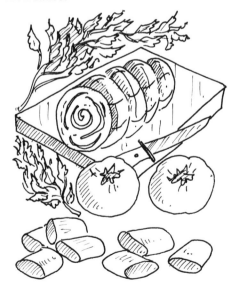

Quadratini with broad beans soup

 About 1 hour

Calories per portion: 433

 Barbarossa rosato (Liguria) (rosé)

For four: *¹/₂ pound quadratini - ¹/₂ pound fresh broad beans - ¹/₄ pound pancetta or bacon - 2 tablespoons olive oil - 8 plum tomatoes - 3 shallot onions - 2 cloves garlic - 1 stalk of celery - 6 basil leaves - ¹/₄ cup chopped parsley - 10 cups of broth (either beef or vegetable broth or stock cubes can be used) - grated Parmesan cheese - salt and pepper.*

Instructions: Dice the pancetta, plum tomatoes, onions, garlic, celery, parsley, and basil leaves. Saute the pancetta in oil a few minutes, then add the diced vegetables and cook 5 minutes, stirring often. Add the tomatoes and herb seasoning and cook 5 more minutes. Shell the beans and add to the sauce and cook 15 minutes. Pour in the broth with seasoning, parsley, and basil and cook for 10 more minutes. Serve in warmed soup bowls and sprinkle with grated cheese.

Maccheroni quadrati with asparagus

 About 1 hour

Calories per portion: 663

 Verdicchio di Matelica (Marche) (white)

For four: *1 pound maccheroni quadrati - 2 pounds of asparagus - 1 clove of garlic (crushed) - 3 tablespoons butter - 4 tablespoons olive oil - 8 plum tomatoes (peeled and diced) - 3 tablespoons cream - grated Parmesan cheese - salt and pepper.*

Instructions: Steam the asparagus, keeping them slightly firm; cut tops of asparagus into 1 inch long pieces. Saute in the butter and oil and garlic for 8 minutes; add the peeled and diced tomatoes and cook for 15 minutes. Pour in the cream, salt and pepper and stir through. Cook and drain the pasta; toss with the Parmesan cheese, then the sauce. Serve immediately.

Maccheroni alla carbonara

 About 25 minutes

Calories per portion: 863

Sangiovese dei Colli Pescaresi (Marche) (red)

For four: *1 pound maccheroni quadrati - ¹/₄ pound lean pancetta or bacon - 4 tablespoons butter - 2 tablespoons olive oil - 4 eggs - 5 tablespoons grated Parmesan cheese - ¹/₂ cup cream - salt and pepper - 3 tablespoons chopped parsley.*

Instructions: Chop the pancetta or bacon into strips; chop the parsley; beat the eggs, cream and Parmesan cheese with the pepper in a mixing bowl. Saute the pancetta in the oil and butter for 8 minutes. Cook and drain the pasta. Transfer to a mixing bowl and stir through quickly, first the cream sauce, then the pancetta with the cooking fat. Serve immediately with the parsley and more cheese, if desired.
(The trick here is to add the egg-cream sauce and stir through the pasta quickly).

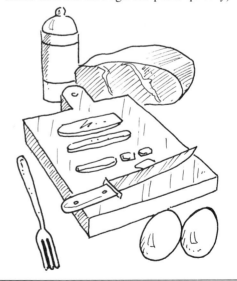

Maccheroni quadrifoglio (Clover leaf Maccheroni)

Also called Quadrifogli
Recommended kind of dough: With eggs - with whole-wheat flour - with durum wheat flour
Cooking time: 7 minutes - 10 minutes - 8 minutes
To be used: Drained (4 ounces per portion)
Variation: Quadrifoglietti. To be used with broth or vegetable soup (2 ounces per portion). Cut the pasta lengthwise into 2" long pieces

Quadrifogli with "Ciociara sauce"

About 1 hour

Calories per portion: 538

Rosso dei Colli del Trasimeno (Umbria) (red)

For four: *1 pound quadrifogli - 1 medium onion - ¹/₄ cup olive oil - ¹/₄ pound pancetta or bacon - 2-3 drops Tabasco sauce - ¹/₄ cup white wine - 3 tablespoons parsley - ¹/₂ pound plum tomatoes - 1 clove garlic - grated Romano cheese - salt and pepper.*

Instructions: Chop the pancetta or bacon, onion, parsley, garlic, and tomatoes.
Saute the pancetta with the onion and garlic in the oil and Tabasco sauce for 2 minutes, pour in the white wine and cook for 5 minutes. Add the tomatoes and cook for 30 minutes. Season with salt and pepper and sprinkle with the parsley. Cook and drain the pasta; toss with the grated cheese and then the sauce.

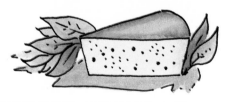

Quadrifoglietti soup, Venetian style

About 1 hour

Calories per portion: 507

Alto Adige Sauvignon (Alto Adige) (white)

For four: *¹/₂ pound quadrifoglietti - ¹/₂ pound plum tomatoes - 3 leeks - ¹/₄ cup chopped parsley - 1 clove garlic - ¹/₂ pound shelled shrimp - 8 cups broth (either vegetable or use stock cubes) - 4 tablespoons olive oil - salt and pepper.*

Instructions: Prepare the leeks - use ends only, slice very fine. Dice the tomatoes, parsley, garlic, and clean the shrimp. Saute the leeks in oil for a few minutes. Add the shrimp, parsley, garlic and chopped tomatoes, then stir and cook for 15 minutes, then transfer to a large pot. Pour in the broth, add pepper and salt and bring to a boil; add the pasta and cook until firm. This soup will be thick, if you prefer a thinner soup, add more water.

146

Quadrifogli with anchovies and chili

 About 20 minutes

Calories per portion: 532

 Ravello rosato (Campania) (rosé)

For four: 1 pound quadrifogli - 6 table-spoons olive oil - 2 cloves garlic - a small piece of chili pepper - 4 anchovy fillets - 4 basil leaves - 3 tablespoons fine bread-crumbs - salt.

Instructions: Chop the garlic, pepper, basil leaves; mash the anchovies. Saute the garlic and chili pepper with the oil, then discard them. To this oil, add the anchovies and basil and cook for a few minutes. Toast the breadcrumbs in a frying pan at high heat, stirring constantly.
Cook and drain the pasta; toss with the sauce, then sprinkle with the toasted breadcrumbs, toss and serve immediately.

Quadrifogli with zucchini

 About 35 minutes

Calories per portion: 504

 Belice bianco (Sicily) (white)

For four: 1 pound quadrifogli - 6 small zucchini - 1 medium onion - 4 tablespoons butter - 2 tablespoons olive oil - 2 eggs - 1/2 cup cream - 4 tablespoons grated Parmesan cheese - 1/4 cup chopped Italian parsley - 1/4 teaspoon Italian herb seasoning - salt and pepper.

Instructions: Wash and slice the zucchini, onion, and parsley. Saute the onion and zucchini in the butter and oil with the herb seasoning, salt and pepper, for 6-8 minutes. Cook and drain the pasta. Beat the eggs in a large bowl with the cream, grated cheese and parsley. Transfer the pasta into the bowl and toss with the egg sauce, then the zucchini sauce. Sprinkle with more grated cheese and serve immediately.

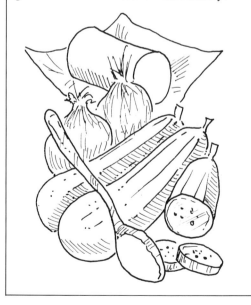

148

Quadrifogli with tuna fish

 About 55 minutes

Calories per portion: 538

Cirò bianco (Calabria) (white)

For four: 1 pound quadrifogli - 1 cup tuna fish (without oil) - ¹/₂ pound plum tomatoes (or 1 cup of tomato sauce) - 1 medium onion - 1 clove garlic - 1 carrot - 1 stalk celery - 4 tablespoons chopped parsley - ¹/₄ cup olive oil - ¹/₂ cup dry white wine - salt and pepper - black olives to decorate.

Instructions: Chop the onion, garlic, carrot, celery, parsley, and tomatoes. Saute all of the vegetables except the tomatoes in oil for 10 minutes; add the tuna fish and wine, stir and cook for 8 minutes. Crush the tomatoes and add to the sauce, stirring frequently; cook for 15 minutes; then season with salt, pepper and chopped parsley. Cook and drain the pasta; toss with the sauce.
This is a great cold dish for the Summer season as well as served hot; decorate with black olives.

Quadrifogli with ricotta cheese

 About 20 minutes

Calories per portion: 512

Sangiovese di Aprilia (Latium) (red)

For four: 1 pound quadrifogli - 1 cup ricotta cheese - 3 tablespoons chopped parsley - 4 tablespoons butter - ¹/₂ cup cream - 4 tablespoons diced basil leaves - 4 tablespoons grated Parmesan cheese - dash of nutmeg - salt and pepper.

Instructions: Soften the butter over low heat for a few minutes, remove from the heat and add the ricotta cheese and the cream; season with salt, pepper, nutmeg and the chopped basil leaves. Cook and drain the pasta; toss with the ricotta sauce and sprinkle with diced parsley and Parmesan cheese.

Sfoglia regolabile per ravioli

(Adjustable wide width for ravioli)

Recommended kind of dough: With eggs
Cooking time: 8-15 minutes (depending on the thickness of the pasta. Indications of cooking times in the single recipes).
To be used: Drained or with broth, for cappelletti, tortellini, ravioli, agnolotti, ravioloni dolci, etc.

Tortellini

  About 1 hour and 30 minutes - plus 105 minutes for the sauce.

Calories per portion: 353

 Barbera dei Colli Bolognesi (Emilia) aged 1-2 years (red)

For four: For the dough: 1 pound plain flour measured in the PastaMatic measuring cup - 4 eggs - 1 tablespoon olive oil.
For the sauce: 1 1/4 pounds of lean beef - 2 cloves of garlic - 2 bayleaves - 2 tablespoons olive oil - 1/2 cup red wine - 1/2 cup tomato puree (or sauce) - 4 tablespoons tomato paste - salt and pepper.
For the filling: 1 pound braised meat - 1/4 pound ham - 1/4 pound sausage - 3 eggs - 4 tablespoons grated Parmesan cheese - pinch of nutmeg - 1 tablespoon olive oil - grated Parmesan cheese for topping.

Instructions: Start with the preparation of the sauce. Saute the meat in the oil with the garlic and bayleaves, turning the meat on all sides to brown. Pour in the wine and cook for 8 minutes. Mix the tomato paste with some boiling water, to thin the paste. Stir until smooth and add to the meat. Cover and cook until the meat is very tender (if you use a CombiVapor pot, it takes only 50 minutes).

Remove the meat and mince. Add to the cooking juices (which you will use as the sauce for the tortellini).
To prepare the filling: skin the sausage and mince with the meat, ham, Parmesan cheese, eggs, nutmeg and stir to mix the ingredients well.
Prepare the dough as instructed in recipe on page 25 (add the flour and eggs to the PastaMatic along with the oil).
Knead for a few minutes until the consistency is right.
Stop the machine and fasten on the disc for sfoglia.
Choose the medium thickness and extrude.
Cut the dough into squares 1 1/2" long.
Put some filling in the center of each square and fold diagonally across, forming a triangle.
Press the borders to stick the ends together.
Bend each triangle around your finger and press one corner over the other.
Bend the central corner outwards, into a small nut shape.
Cook the tortellini a few minutes in boiling water, with a few drops of oil.
Drain and toss with the minced meat sauce and then the grated Parmesan cheese.
Serve immediately.

Piadina

20 minutes - plus time necessary for the dough to rise (2 hours) and for cooking the piadine (3-4 minutes each)

Calories per portion: 470

Lambrusco di Sorbara (Emilia) (red)

For six: *1 pound plain flour measured in the PastaMatic measuring cup - 1 egg - 1 grated lemon peel - ¹/₂ teaspoon baking powder - 2 tablespoons lard - milk and water in the PastaMatic liquid measuring cup up to the level for "1 pound" on the water side.*

Instructions: Pour the flour, grated lemon peel, baking powder and lard into the PastaMatic bowl, and allow the ingredients to knead for a few minutes.
Add the egg and mixture of milk and water. Knead for 5 minutes and then turn off the PastaMatic and allow the dough to rise for 2 hours.
Turn on the machine and allow some dough to extrude.
Turn off the PastaMatic and fasten on the sfoglia disc.
Turn the machine on and cut the dough into squares and lie on the kitchen board sprinkled with flour, to dry.
To cook the piadine, use a thick-bottom, non-stick frying pan.
When the pan is hot, lay a piadina on the bottom, rotate the piece of dough, punching it with a fork.
When the piadina is done on one side, roll it to the other side and rotate and puncture with a fork.
Allow the piadina to get slightly toasted, depending on the heat, it will take 3-4 minutes.

Toast the piadine, one at a time.
You can serve them plain or with cream, melted cheese, ham or even marmalade.
You can even cut the piadina into halves and stuff with many different types of fillings... very versatile and fun!

Tortellini baked in cream sauce

 About 45 minutes

Calories per portion: 373

Lambrusco Reggiano (Emilia) (red)

For four: 1 pound tortellini (see tortellini recipe on page 150) - 1 tablespoon olive oil - 1 cup cream - 3 tablespoons of dry Marsala wine - 2 tablespoons of butter - grated Parmesan cheese - pepper.

Instructions: Cook the tortellini in boiling water with a few drops of oil (to keep from sticking). Drain, after a few minutes (still firm to the bite), grease a baking pan with butter and lay the tortellini, arranged on small spits, on the bottom of the pan. Cover with the cream and sprinkle with the Marsala wine and with the grated cheese. Bake for 10 minutes at 350 °F.

Ravioli with cheese

 About 1 hour - plus time to allow the filling to rest

Calories per portion: 872

Breganze bianco (Venetia) (white)

For six: 1 pound of dough with eggs (see tortellini recipe on page 150), medium thickness - grated Parmesan cheese.
For the filling: ¹/₂ cup grated Parmesan cheese - 5 ounces diced Italian fontina cheese - 2 eggs - 2 egg whites - pinch of nutmeg - salt and pepper.
To cook: 10 cups of meat broth - 1 egg, to spread over the pasta with a brush.

Instructions: Mix the ingredients for the filling until the texture is smooth. Set aside for 30 minutes in the refrigerator. Prepare the dough and cut into 13" long strips. Lay the strips of dough on a kitchen cloth, sprinkled with flour and cover with another kitchen cloth to prevent them from becoming too dry. Thin the egg with 1 tablespoon of water. Brush half the strips of dough with the egg mixture. Place a small amount of filling on each piece of dough, making two lines and arranging the small balls of filling about 1" apart from one another. Cover each strip of dough with filling, and another strip of dough. Press the borders together to seal around the filling. Cut the dough widthwise into little squares with a fluted pastry wheel. Lay the ravioli on a kitchen towel spread with flour, without overlapping. Cook the ravioli with the broth over low heat for about 10 minutes. Season with salt and pepper and grated Parmesan cheese.

Ravioli au gratin

   About 2 hours

Calories per portion: 803

Frecciarossa bianco dell'Oltrepò Pavese (Lombardy) (white)

For six: 1 pound dough with eggs, medium thickness (see tortellini recipe on page 150).
For the filling: 1/2 pound Italian sweet or hot sausage - 2 tablespoons olive oil - 3 shallot onions - 4 tablespoons chopped parsley - 1 tablespoon fine breadcrumbs - 3 tablespoons grated Parmesan cheese - 2 egg yolks - pinch of nutmeg - salt and pepper - 1 egg to brush over the pasta with a kitchen brush.
For the sauce: 2 tablespoons butter - 3 tablespoons grated Parmesan cheese - 1/2 cup cream - salt and pepper.

Instructions: Filling: chop the onions, parsley and sausage (which should be skinned and crushed). Saute the onions in the oil, until golden brown. Add the sausage and cook for 15 minutes. Mix the egg yolks and blend into the sausage mixture with the breadcrumbs and grated cheese, seasoned with the nutmeg and salt and pepper. Mix and prepare the ravioli (as instructed on page 153 under "Ravioli with cheese"). Brush the dough with the egg mixture. Lay the small pieces of filling 1 1/2" apart and seal the ends. Cook the ravioli for about 15 minutes and drain, then transfer into a baking pan (greased with butter) alternating the layers of ravioli with melted butter, salt and pepper and grated cheese and cream. Bake until the surface gets a golden color and crusty at 350 °F for about 10 minutes.

Ravioli with zucchini

  About 1 hour and 30 minutes - plus time necessary to cook the zucchini

Calories per portion: 850

Pomino bianco (Tuscany) (white)

For six: 1 pound of dough with eggs, medium thickness (see recipe for tortellini on page 150).
For the filling: 2 pounds of zucchini - 3 ounces grated Parmesan cheese - 6 macaroons - pinch of nutmeg - 1 tablespoon of honey - 1 grated lemon peel - 1 egg to brush over the pasta with a kitchen brush.
For the sauce: 3 tablespoons of butter - 2 tablespoons of grated Romano cheese - 5 sage leaves, crushed, or 1/4 teaspoon dried sage leaves.

Instructions: Preparation of the filling: peel and chop the zucchini and bake for 20 minutes at 350 °F (until soft and golden in color). Transfer to a mixing bowl and crush with a fork. Add the macaroons, nutmeg, honey, lemon peel, and cheese. Blend the ingredients until smooth. Prepare the ravioli (see page 153 recipe for "Ravioli with cheese"). Lay small pieces of filling 1 1/2" apart on the dough strips. Cover with another strip, brush with egg mixture and seal the ends. Cook and drain the ravioli. Coat with the grated cheese and butter that has been cooked with the sage leaves.

Sweet ravioli with marmalade

 About 30 minutes - plus time to fry the ravioli

Calories per portion: 855 for 6 ravioli

 Lachrima Christi bianco (Campania) (white)

For six: for the dough: ¹/₂ *pound plain flour measured in the PastaMatic measuring cup - 3 tablespoons sugar - 1 egg - ¹/₂ tablespoon Nocello liqueur - 3 tablespoons of milk - 1 tablespoon olive oil - ¹/₄ teaspoon baking powder - 3 tablespoons powdered sugar.*
For filling: 1 cup of cherry, orange or apricot marmalade.
Oil for frying.

Instructions: Pour the flour, sugar, and baking powder into the PastaMatic bowl and knead for 1 minute. Mix the egg with the liqueur, milk and oil and pour through the opening of the lid, using the liquid measuring cup. Knead for 5 minutes. Remove the slide and extrude some dough. Turn off the PastaMatic and fasten the disc for sfoglia. Turn on the PastaMatic and cut the dough into 13" long strips. Use a glass or pastry mold to cut the strips of dough into round pieces. Brush the pieces with the beaten egg, using a kitchen brush. Lay some marmalade in the center, and cover with a dough strip and press the borders together to seal. Continue, until all the dough has been used. Fry the sweet ravioli in abundant hot oil - a few at a time-until golden brown. Drain and lay the ravioli on paper towels. Sprinkle with powder sugar and serve hot.

Shepherd's ravioli

 About 1 hour and 30 minutes

Calories per portion: 838

Lambrusco di Sorbara (Emilia) (red)

For six: 1 pound of dough with eggs, medium thickness (see recipe for tortellini on page 150).
For the filling: 1 cup of beets - 1 cup ricotta cheese - 2 tablespoons grated Parmesan cheese - 1 egg and 1 egg yolk - pinch of nutmeg - salt and pepper - 1 egg to brush on the dough with a kitchen brush.
For the sauce: 2 ounces butter - 3 tablespoons grated Parmesan cheese - 1 cup cream.

Instructions: Wash and cook the beets. Chop and mix with the ricotta cheese, Parmesan cheese and the remaining ingredients. Blend thoroughly. Prepare the ravioli as mentioned on page 153. Brush the dough with the egg using a kitchen brush. Place small amounts of filling about 2" apart, to get larger ravioli. Cook in boiling water for 15 minutes over medium heat. Drain and sprinkle with grated cheese. Heat the butter and mix with the cream and pour over the ravioli.

Agnolotti soup
with giblets

 About 1 hour and 30 minutes

Calories per portion: 814

 Casteller (Trentino) (red)

For six: ¹/₂ *pound of dough with eggs, small thickness (see tortellini recipe on page 150).*
For the filling: ¹/₂ *pound chicken giblets - 2 tablespoons butter -* ¹/₄ *pound ham - 2 tablespoons grated Parmesan cheese - 1 bayleaf - 1 egg - pinch of cinnamon powder - salt and pepper.*
To cook: 12 cups of meat broth - 1 egg to brush over dough.

Instructions: Boil the chicken giblets, then chop and saute with the oil and bayleaf. Chop the ham and add the grated cheese, egg, cinnamon and salt. Mix all the ingredients together and blend well.
Prepare the agnolotti as instructed on page 153 for "Ravioli with cheese". Brush the dough with the egg, and place small amounts of filling about 1¹/₂" apart. Cover with another piece of dough, close ends by pressing together. Boil the agnolotti in the broth and cook for 10 minutes. Sprinkle with grated cheese and serve immediately.

Flat loaf with cheese

 About 1 hour and 20 minutes

Calories per portion: 837

 Albana di Romagna Amabile or Dole (white)

For four: For the dough: ¹/₂ *pound plain flour measured in the PastaMatic measuring cup - 3 tablespoons butter - 3 egg yolks - milk.*
For the filling: 1 ¹/₂ *cups of ricotta cheese - 2 tablespoons milk - dash of nutmeg - pinch of sugar - salt and pepper - oil (for baking pan).*

Instructions: Pour the flour, butter (softened and cut into small pieces) into the PastaMatic bowl. Knead for 2 minutes and add the egg and milk mixture (measured in the liquid measuring cup up to the egg level for "¹/₂ pound flour"). Pour through the opening in the lid. Knead for 5 minutes. Remove the slide and extrude some dough. Turn off the PastaMatic and fasten on the disc, preheated in hot water. Turn the PastaMatic on and extrude the dough. Cut the dough lengthwise into pieces as long as needed to place the strips of dough side by side in a baking pan, 8 x 10" (greased with butter). Arrange the strips of dough to cover a part of the sides of the baking pan in a box-like shape. Now prepare the filling: thin the cheese with milk and season with the nutmeg, salt and pepper. Spread over the dough, except the borders, and cover with the remaining strips of dough. Press with your fingers to seal. Puncture the surface with a fork and bake in a hot oven (350 °F) for 40 minutes. Serve either hot or cold.

Easter pie

  About 2 hours and 15 minutes

Calories per portion: 503

Pigato di Albenga (Liguria) (white)

For six: For the dough: ¹/₂ *pound plain flour measured in the PastaMatic measuring cup - 2 eggs - 1 tablespoon olive oil -* ¹/₂ *cup cream - 3 tablespoons grated Parmesan cheese - pinch of nutmeg - butter - olive oil and 4 tablespoons for baking - salt and pepper.*
For the filling: 2 pounds beets - 1 cup Italian ricotta cheese - 5 eggs.

Instructions: Prepare the dough as usual, using the above mentioned ingredients, but add the oil just after the eggs. Extrude the dough through the medium thickness sfoglia disc and cut it lengthwise into 12" long strips. Place the strips on the kitchen board, sprinkled with flour. Cover with a wet kitchen towel.
Prepare the filling: wash the beet leaves, drain and half cook them in a covered pot with water. Drain and chop. Mix the ricotta cheese with 1 egg, cream, grated cheese, the beets and seasoning. Grease a baking pan with butter and sprinkle with flour. Use half the strips of dough to cover the bottom and the side walls of the baking pan. Overlap the strips slightly and press together with your fingers. Pour the filling on the dough, making an even amount with a spoon. Make four holes in the filling and pour in the remaining eggs and a small piece of butter in each space.
Sprinkle with grated cheese, salt and pepper. Top the pie with the remaining strips of dough and press with your fingers to seal. Spread with olive oil and puncture the surface. Bake in a hot oven at 350 °F for 1 hour.

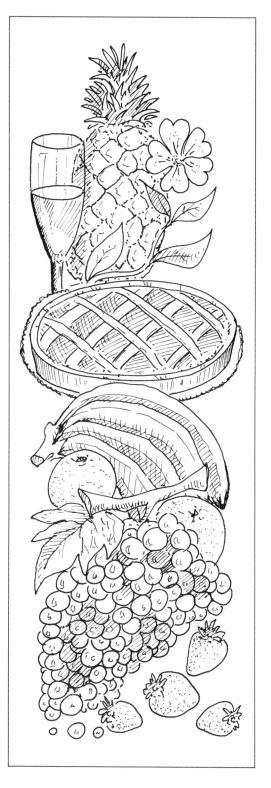

Colored pastas

Colored pastas are a novelty and they will bring more joy and versatility to your cooking. We are not only proposing the usual green pasta with spinach (which you may also find in a box), but a whole range of different colors, unusual tastes, plus a higher nutritional value due to the fresh ingredients. Generally vegetables which are rich in vitamins and minerals are added to the dough.

The following is an extensive range of recipes, to offer you more versatility and stimulate your creativity: invent your own pasta creations!

Technical suggestions:

1. When you use vegetables which need to be pre-cooked, do not boil them with water, but steam or bake them in the oven (as instructed for each single case).

2. Colored pastas, containing vegetables and a lower number of eggs than usual, require a decrease by 2-3 minutes in cooking time recommended for the corresponding shape of standard pasta.

Pasta with spinach

 About 35 minutes

Calories per portion: 259

For four: *1 pound plain flour measured in the PastaMatic measuring cup - ¹/₂ pound fresh spinach (use leaves only) - 2 eggs.*

Instructions: Wash, and steam cook the spinach and drain well. Pour the flour, and spinach into the PastaMatic bowl and begin kneading. Pour the first egg and second yolk through the opening in the lid, using the liquid egg cup. Knead for five minutes and add the second egg white. When the dough is the proper consistency remove the slide and extrude some dough. Turn off the PastaMatic and fasten on the disc. Turn on the PastaMatic and extrude the dough.

Recommended shapes: all kinds of tagliatelle, sfoglia, and adjustable wide width for ravioli, conchigliette rigate.

Pasta with spinach "Farmer's wife style"

Pasta with spinach "Farmer's wife style"

 About 1 hour

Calories per portion: 623

 Vesuvio rosso aged 1 year (Campania) (red)

For four: 1 pound spinach pasta - 1 onion - 4 tablespoons olive oil - 2 tablespoons butter - 2 bayleaves - 1 pound rabbit meat - 1/2 cup dry white wine - 1 cup tomato puree or sauce - 1/2 cup broth (stock cubes can be used, beef or vegetable) - 1/4 cup chopped parsley - grated Parmesan cheese - salt and pepper.

Instructions: Chop the onion, rabbit meat, parsley and bayleaves. Saute the rabbit meat with onion, bayleaves, and seasoning in the oil for 15 minutes. Pour in the wine and allow to cook for 10 minutes; add the tomato puree and broth and cook for 40 minutes.
Cook and drain the pasta.
Sprinkle with the grated cheese and toss with the sauce.

Green pasta with wild mushrooms

 About 50 minutes

Calories per portion: 658

 Merlot del Trentino (Trentino) (red)

For four: 1 pound spinach pasta (in your favorite shape) - 1 pound wild mushrooms - 2 cloves of garlic - 3 tablespoons diced parsley - 1 stock cube (beef or vegetable) - 1/4 cup olive oil - 1 cup cream - grated Parmesan cheese - salt and pepper.

Instructions: Wash and slice the mushrooms, dice the garlic and parsley. Heat the garlic in the oil, when golden colored, discard. Add the mushrooms and saute for 6 minutes. Pour in the stock cube and a cup of hot water, adding gradually. When practically done, add the parsley and seasoning. Cook and drain the pasta and transfer into a large mixing bowl (preheated). Add the cream, grated cheese and the mushroom sauce and toss through.

Pasta with Swiss chard

 About 35 minutes

Calories per portion: 270

For four: 1 pound of plain flour measured in the PastaMatic measuring cup - 3 ounces Swiss chard (use the tender leaves and tops only), 3 eggs.

Instructions: Wash and steam cook the Swiss chard. Drain and chop the tops and leaves; add to the PastaMatic bowl with the flour. Turn on the PastaMatic and pour in the eggs. Follow the instructions for the basic dough with eggs (see page 25). You will obtain a darker and more easily digestible and richer pasta than spinach pasta.
Recommended shapes: all sizes of tagliatelle, sfoglia and adjustable wide width for ravioli, conchigliette rigate.

Pasta with Swiss chard and mozzarella cheese

 About 35 minutes

Calories per portion: 657

 Federico II rosato (Apulia) (rosé)

For four: 1 pound of pasta with Swiss chard - 4 tablespoons of butter - 1/2 pound plum tomatoes - 8 basil leaves - 1/2 pound mozzarella cheese - 3 tablespoons of cream - grated Parmesan cheese - salt and pepper.

Instructions: Chop the tomatoes, basil, salt, pepper and mozzarella cheese. Cook the tomatoes in the butter for 15 minutes. Mix in the cream, diced mozzarella and chopped basil and cook for a few minutes. Remove from heat, and stir constantly until the cheese melts and the texture is smooth. Cook and drain the pasta. Sprinkle with the grated cheese, then toss with the sauce and serve immediately.

Pasta with nettles

  About 35 minutes

Calories per portion: 272

Bardolino classico (Venetia) (red)

For four: *1 pound flour - (measured in the PastaMatic measuring cup) - 4 ounces nettles (use the tender leaves and the tops only) - 3 eggs.*

Instructions: Compared with spinach, nettles are tastier and contain less water. Therefore they do not make the pasta too soft and you can get better results and more pasta using them.
Wash, steam-cook the nettles and drain. Chop the nettles and pour with the flour into the PastaMatic bowl. Turn on the PastaMatic and pour in the eggs through the opening of the lid (add the third white of the eggs only if necessary). Follow the instructions for the basic dough with eggs (see page 25).(You will obtain a darker but more easily digestible and richer pasta).
Recommended shapes: all kinds of tagliatelle - sfoglia - adjustable wide width for ravioli.

Tomato pasta

  About 10 minutes

Calories per portion: 266

For five: *1 pound plain flour measured in the PastaMatic measuring cup - 3 ounces tomato extract or paste (from a tube) - 2 eggs.*

Instructions: Pour the flour and tomato extract into the PastaMatic bowl and knead. After 2 minutes, add the eggs slowly through the opening of the lid. Check the consistency of the dough and follow the instructions for the basic dough with eggs (see page 25).
Recommended shapes: spaghetti, small spaghetti, chitarre, bucatini, bucati rigati, penne, maccheroni, farmer's pasta, maccheroni quadrati, maccheroni quadrifoglio.

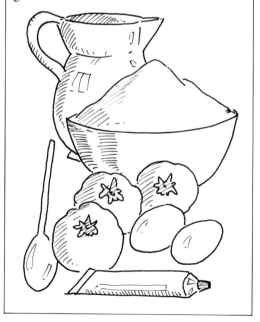

Mushroom soup with tomato pasta

 About 1 hour

Calories per portion: 270

 Pinot nero (Trentino) (red)

For four: *1/2 pound tomato pasta (cut into 2" long pieces) - 1/2 pound fresh mushrooms - 1 medium onion - 3 tablespoons chopped parsley - 1 clove of garlic - 9 cups of broth (stock cubes may be used - chicken or beef) - grated Parmesan cheese - salt and pepper.*

Instructions: Slice the mushrooms, onion, parsley and garlic and add to a large cooking pot. Saute in the oil for 8 minutes. Add the broth and bring to a boil. Add the tomato pasta and cook until firm. Season with salt and pepper and add the grated cheese to each serving bowl.

Pasta with red beets

 About 15 minutes

Calories per portion: 283

For five: *1 pound plain flour measured in the PastaMatic measuring cup - 1/2 cup finely chopped red beets - 2 eggs.*

Instructions: Wash, peel and chop the red beets very finely and add with the flour to the PastaMatic bowl. Turn on the Pasta-Matic and pour in 1 egg and 1 egg yolk through the opening of the lid. If the dough is too dry (the beets contain a great deal of water), add the white of the second egg. Follow the instructions for the basic dough with eggs (see page 25). The pasta with red beets is a dark, wine color (the color will fade slightly during the cooking process).
Recommended shapes: bucati rigati, bucatini, bucati, conchigliette rigate, farmer's pasta, maccheroni quadrati, maccheroni quadrifoglio.

Pasta with red beets and four kinds of cheese

 About 15 minutes

Calories per portion: 662

 Custoza bianco (Venetia) (white)

For four: 1 pound of pasta with red beets - 2 tablespoons of butter - ¼ pound Italian fontina cheese - 1 ounces of gorgonzola cheese - 3 ounces of mozzarella cheese - ½ cup of cream - pinch of grated nutmeg - salt pepper and grated Parmesan cheese.

Instructions: Melt the butter in a large frying pan. Add the diced cheeses and cream and stir. Allow the cheese to melt. Season with nutmeg, salt and pepper. Remove from heat and continue stirring. Cook the pasta and drain. Transfer to the frying pan and stir through the cheese sauce. Allow the pasta to absorb the cheese sauce perfectly. Sprinkle with grated Parmesan cheese.

Pasta with cocoa

 About 15 minutes

Calories per portion: 281

For five: 1 pound plain flour measured in the PastaMatic measuring cup - 2 full tablespoons bitter cocoa - 4 eggs - 1 egg white - dash of salt.

Instructions: Pour the flour, cocoa and salt into the PastaMatic bowl and mix the ingredients well. Add the eggs slowly through the opening of the lid, using the PastaMatic liquid egg cup. Pour in the white of the egg. Knead for 5 minutes and when the ingredients are perfectly kneaded, follow the instructions for the basic dough with eggs (see page 25).
Recommended shapes: all kinds of tagliatelle.

Cocoa tagliatelle with Würstel sausage sauce

  About 15 minutes

Calories per portion: 763

No wine recommended; it is advisable to drink beer

For four: *1 pound cocoa tagliatelle - 6 skinned Würstel (hot dogs or sausages can be used in place of the German sausages) - 2 tablespoons of butter - 1 tablespoon Worcester sauce - ¹/₂ teaspoon mild paprika - 1 cup of cream - grated Parmesan cheese - salt.*

Instructions: Finely slice the Würstel and saute in the butter for 5 minutes. Sprinkle with the Worcester sauce and add the paprika and the cream. Stir and allow to thicken a few minutes. Cook the cocoa tagliatelle and drain. Toss with the grated Parmesan cheese and pour the sauce over the pasta, and toss through.

Zucchini pasta

  About 40 minutes

Calories per portion: 240

Cortese di Gavi (Piedmont) (white)

Ingredients: *1 pound plain flour measured in the PastaMatic measuring cup - ¹/₂ pound fresh zucchini - 2 eggs - grated Parmesan cheese - 2 tablespoons of butter.*

Instructions: Peel, slice and bake the zucchini in low heat until soft. Mash the zucchini until smooth. Pour into the PastaMatic bowl. Turn on the PastaMatic and add the eggs through the opening in the lid using the PastaMatic liquid cup. Knead for 6 minutes. Remove the slide and extrude some dough. Turn off the PastaMatic and fasten on the disc. Turn on the PastaMatic and extrude the pasta desired. Cook and drain the pasta. Toss with melted butter and grated Parmesan cheese in order to taste the zucchini.
Recommended shapes: all types of large, hollow pasta.

Carrot pasta

About 30 minutes

Calories per portion: 284

Ingredients: *1 pound plain flour measured in the PastaMatic measuring cup - ¹/₂ pound carrots - 2 egg yolks.*

Instructions: Steam cook the carrots and chop very finely. Pour the flour, eggs and carrots into the PastaMatic bowl, using the PastaMatic liquid cup. Knead for 5 minutes and remove the slide and extrude some dough. Fasten on the disc (preheated with hot water). Turn on the PastaMatic and extrude the dough.
Recommended shapes: spaghettoni, chitarre, bucatini, bucati rigati, penne, maccheroni.

Chitarre with carrot "Autumn style"

About 50 minutes

Calories per portion: 534

Castellana Grotte rosato (Apulia) (rosé)

For four: *1 pound chitarre with carrot - ¹/₂ pound plum tomatoes - ¹/₄ cup dried mushrooms - 4 tablespoons olive oil - 2 cloves of garlic - ¹/₂ cup cream - salt and pepper - grated Parmesan cheese.*

Instructions: Soak the mushrooms in cold water for one hour. Chop and saute with the crushed garlic in the oil for 15 minutes. Add the chopped plum tomatoes, salt and pepper and cook for 20 minutes. Add the cream, and cook for 5 minutes, stirring constantly. Cook the pasta and drain. Sprinkle with the grated cheese and toss. Pour the sauce over the pasta and toss through. Serve immediately.

Pasta prepared with the juices of fresh fruits, vegetables and with herbs

Orange flavored pasta

 About 20 minutes

Calories per portion: 272

 No wine - it does not blend well with citrus fruit

For five: *1 pound plain flour measured in the PastaMatic measuring cup - 2 eggs - 2 orange peels (grated) - orange juice.*

Instructions: Pour the flour into the PastaMatic bowl. Turn on the PastaMatic and add the eggs, using the liquid measuring cup. Fill the liquid measuring cup with orange juice and the peel to the mark for "1 pound of flour" on the egg side. Add to the PastaMatic and knead for 6 minutes. Remove the slide and extrude some dough. Turn off the PastaMatic and fasten on the disc. Extrude the pasta.
Orange-flavored pasta requires 1-2 minutes less than normal cooking time. An orange sauce is recommended with this type of pasta or cream sauce.
Recommended shapes: spaghetti, linguine, tagliatelle, chitarre, or bucatini.

Bucatini with orange sauce

 About 20 minutes

Calories per portion: 551

 No wine recommended

For four: *1 pound orange flavored bucatini - 1 orange (use the juice) - 1 tablespoon corn starch - 2 tablespoons cognac or brandy - pinch of nutmeg - 3 tablespoons butter - 4 tablespoons cream - grated Romano cheese - grated orange peel.*

Instructions: Melt the corn starch with the orange juice. Add the cognac, nutmeg and grated orange peel and cook for a few minutes.
Use a small frying pan and melt the butter and the cream. Add the orange mixture and simmer, stirring often and remove from the heat. Cook the bucatini and drain. Sprinkle with the cheese and toss with the orange sauce.

Strawberry-flavored pasta

 About 20 minutes plus time necessary to drain the fruits

Calories per portion: 223

Lambrusco di Sorbara (Emilia) (red)

For five: For the dough: 1 pound plain flour measured in the PastaMatic measuring cup - ¼ cup strawberry pulp - 2 eggs For the sauce: 3 tablespoons butter - Romano cheese, grated.

Instructions: Wash and dice the fruit and place in the BravoSimac and puree. Put the puree through a sieve to remove excess juice and water. Fill the PastaMatic liquid measuring cup with fruit puree to the mark for "1 pound" on the egg level side. Pour into the PastaMatic bowl and add the flour. Knead for 2 minutes, then add the slightly beaten eggs through the opening of the lid, using the liquid measuring cup. When the ingredients are perfectly mixed, remove the slide and extrude some dough. Turn off the PastaMatic and fasten on the disc. Turn on the PastaMatic and extrude the pasta. Cook the pasta and drain (reducing the cooking time by 2 minutes).
A plain sauce is recommended in order to taste the delicious flavor of the pasta. A simple sauce of just melted butter and light Romano cheese, or a light cream and nutmeg sauce.
Recommended shapes: spaghetti, small spaghetti, chitarre.

Artichoke-flavored pasta

 About 50 minutes

Calories per portion: 224

Cortese di Gavi (Piedmont) (white)

For five: For the dough: 1 pound plain flour measured in the PastaMatic measuring cup - 3 artichokes (use the hearts only) - 2 eggs.
For the sauce: 3 tablespoons butter - grated Parmesan cheese.

Instructions: Snap off the green, hard leaves from the artichokes, use the hearts only. Chop into quarters and steam cook. Press through a food mill. Pour the flour and the artichoke puree into the PastaMatic bowl. Knead for a few minutes. Add the eggs through the opening of the lid. Knead for 6 minutes and remove the slide and extrude some dough. Turn off the PastaMatic and fasten on the disc. Extrude the pasta.
Cook the pasta and drain (reducing the cooking time by 1-2 minutes). Toss with the grated cheese and melted butter. This is the simplest and best way to compliment the artichoke pasta, to fully appreciate the wonderful artichoke flavor.

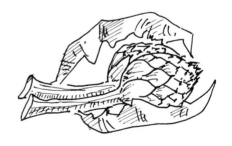

Wild Mushroom flavored pasta

  About 15 minutes - plus time to soak the mushrooms

Calories per portion: 301

Cabernet del Trentino (Trentino-Alto Adige) aged 1-2 years (red)

For five: For the dough: 1 pound of plain flour measured in the PastaMatic measuring cup - 3 ounces dried, wild mushrooms - 1 egg - 2 egg whites.
For the sauce: 2 tablespoons butter - grated Parmesan cheese.

Instructions: Soak the mushrooms for an hour in lukewarm water. Chop the mushrooms very finely. Pour the flour and the mushrooms into the PastaMatic bowl. Knead for 2 minutes. Add the egg through the opening of the lid and then pour in the egg whites, gradually. When the dough is the right consistency, remove the slide and extrude some dough. Turn off the PastaMatic and fasten on the disc. Extrude the pasta.
Cook the pasta and drain. Sprinkle with the grated cheese and toss with melted butter or light cream sauce. Reduce the cooking time by 2 minutes, as the pasta is very delicate.
Recommended shapes: all kinds of tagliatelle.

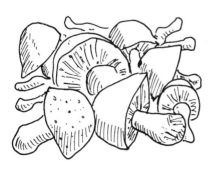

Basil-flavored pasta

  About 20 minutes

Calories per portion: 283

Cirò bianco (Calabria) (white)

For five: For the dough: 1 pound flour (measured in the PastaMatic measuring cup) - 3 ounces basil leaves - 3 eggs.
For the topping: 3 ounces butter - grated Parmesan cheese.

Instructions: Pour the flour and the basil leaves (washed and finely chopped) into the PastaMatic bowl and knead for a couple of minutes. Add the eggs through the opening of the lid. Knead for 5-6 minutes and when the dough has reached the proper consistency, remove the slide and extrude some dough, which you will put back into the bowl. Turn off the PastaMatic and fasten on the disc, preheated with hot water. Cook the pasta in abundant, salted water, drain when firm to the bite, and sprinkle with the grated Parmesan cheese. Melt the fresh butter over low heat and pour over the pasta.
This is the simplest and yet the best way to serve the basil-flavored pasta, emphasizing its unique taste. Reduce the cooking time of any shape of pasta by 1-2 minutes, when using the basil-flavored dough.
Recommended shapes: all kinds of tagliatelle and the bucati.

Garlic-flavored pasta

 About 15 minutes

Calories per portion: 285

 Etna bianco (Sicily) (white)

For six: For the dough: 1 pound plain flour measured in the PastaMatic measuring cup - 1 ounce crushed garlic - 4 eggs.
For the sauce: 2 tablespoons of butter or oil - grated Parmesan cheese.

Instructions: Use a garlic crusher and crush the garlic. Pour the flour and the garlic mixture into the PastaMatic bowl and knead. Add the eggs through the opening of the lid, using the liquid measuring cup. Knead for 6 minutes. Remove the slide and extrude some dough. Turn off the PastaMatic and fasten on the disc. Extrude the pasta. Cook the pasta and drain. Sprinkle with the grated cheese and add the melted butter or oil and toss through.
Recommended shapes: spaghettoni, chitarre, bucati rigati, bucatini, farmer's pasta.

Pesto sauce flavored pasta

 About 25 minutes

Calories per portion: 225

Cortese dell'Oltrepò Pavese (Lombardy) (white)

For five: For the dough: 1 pound plain flour measured in the PastaMatic measuring cup - 15 basil leaves - 2 cloves garlic - 2 eggs - 3 tablespoons pine nuts.
For the sauce: 2 tablespoons butter - grated Romano cheese - 1 clove of garlic.

Instructions: Wash and dry the basil leaves and chop with the garlic and pine nuts. Pour the flour and the basil mixture into the PastaMatic bowl. Knead for 2 minutes and add the slightly beaten eggs through the opening of the lid, using the liquid measuring cup.
When the ingredients are the right consistency, remove the slide and extrude some dough. Turn off the PastaMatic and fasten on the disc. Cut the pasta. Cook the pasta (reducing the cooking time by 2 minutes) and drain. Melt the butter with the crushed clove of garlic and pour over the pasta and sprinkle with the grated Romano cheese and toss through.
Recommended shapes: spaghetti, spaghettoni, chitarre, linguine and tagliatelle.

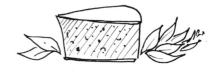

Onion-flavored pasta

 About 15 minutes

Calories per portion: 275

 Gutturnio dei Colli Piacentini (Emilia) aged 2 years (red)

For five: *For the dough: 1 pound plain flour measured into the PastaMatic measuring cup - 3 medium onions - 2 eggs.*
For the sauce: 2 tablespoons of butter - grated Parmesan cheese.

Instructions: Chop the onions. Pour the flour and the chopped onions into the PastaMatic bowl. Knead and add the eggs through the opening in the lid, using the liquid measuring cup. Knead for 5 minutes. Remove the slide and extrude some dough. Turn off the PastaMatic and fasten on the disc. Cut the pasta according to the desired length. Cook and drain the pasta. Sprinkle with grated Parmesan cheese and toss with the melted butter.
Recommended shapes: spaghetti, chitarre, tagliatelle, linguine, bucatini.

Pine nut flavored pasta

 About 15 minutes

Calories per portion: 346

 Rossese di Dolceacqua (Liguria) (red)

For five: *For the dough: 1 pound plain flour - 5 ounces pine nuts - 4 eggs.*
For the sauce: 2 tablespoons butter - grated Parmesan cheese.

Instructions: Chop the pine nuts very finely. Pour the flour and the pine nuts into the PastaMatic bowl and knead for 2 minutes. Add the eggs, using the liquid measuring cup. Knead for 5 minutes. Remove the slide and extrude some dough. Turn off the PastaMatic and fasten on the disc. Extrude the pasta. Cook and drain the pasta. Sprinkle with the grated cheese and pour the melted butter over the pasta and toss.

Parsley-flavored pasta

 About 15 minutes

Calories per portion: 277

For five: 1 pound plain flour measured in the PastaMatic measuring cup - ¹/₂ cup diced parsley leaves - 2 eggs.

Instructions: Wash, drain, and chop the parsley leaves, very finely. Pour the flour and the chopped parsley into the Pasta-Matic bowl and knead for a few minutes. Add the eggs through the opening of the lid, using the liquid measuring cup. Knead for 6 minutes. Remove the slide and extrude some dough. Turn off the PastaMatic and fasten on the disc. Extrude the pasta. Cook and drain the pasta. Use a cream, cheese, or olive and anchovy sauce with the parsley-flavored pasta. Reduce the cooking time by 2 minutes.
Recommended shapes: all kinds of small pasta shapes.

Linguine with olive and anchovy sauce

 About 25 minutes

Calories per portion: 496

 Rossese di Albenga (Liguria) aged 1 year (red)

For four: 1 pound small parsley - flavored tagliatelle - 2 tablespoons olive oil - 1 clove garlic - 3 tablespoons parsley - 4 flat anchovies - 1 cup chopped plum tomatoes - 10 green olives - ¹/₄ teaspoon Italian herb seasoning - salt and pepper - grated Romano cheese.

Instructions: Chop the garlic, parsley, olives (pitted), tomatoes and anchovies. Saute the garlic in the oil for a few minutes, then add the anchovies and stir through. Add the tomatoes, herb seasoning and the olives and cook for 10 minutes.
Season with the parsley, salt and pepper. Cook the pasta and drain. Sprinkle with the grated cheese and toss with the sauce.

178

Anchovy-flavored pasta

  About 10 minutes

Calories per portion: 303

Müller Thurgau (Trentino-Alto Adige) (white)

For five: For the dough: 1 pound plain flour measured in the PastaMatic measuring cup - 2 eggs - 4 tablespoons anchovy paste.
For the sauce: 2 tablespoons butter - grated Parmesan cheese.

Instructions: Pour the flour and the anchovy paste into the PastaMatic bowl and knead for 2 minutes. Add the eggs and knead for 5 minutes. Remove the slide and extrude some dough. Turn off the PastaMatic and fasten on the disc. Extrude the pasta. Cook and drain the pasta (reduce the cooking time by 2 minutes). Toss with the grated Parmesan cheese and melted butter.
Recommended shapes: fili d'oro, capellini, spaghetti, linguine, tagliatelle.

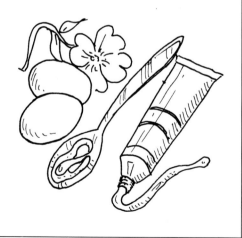

Black olive-flavored pasta

  About 15 minutes

Calories per portion: 312

Pomino bianco (Tuscany) (white)

For five: For the dough: 1 pound plain flour measured in the PastaMatic measuring cup - 10 black olives - 2 eggs - 2 egg yolks.
For the sauce: 2 tablespoons of butter - grated Parmesan cheese.

Instructions: Pit the olives and chop into a pulp texture. Pour the olive pulp and the flour into the PastaMatic bowl and knead. Add the eggs through the opening of the lid, using the liquid measuring cup. Knead for 6 minutes and remove the slide. Extrude some dough and turn off the PastaMatic. Fasten on the disc. Extrude the pasta. Cook and drain the pasta (reduce cooking time by 2 minutes). Use the melted butter and grated cheese as a sauce for the pasta.
Recommended shapes: spaghetti, small spaghetti, chitarre, linguine, tagliatelle.

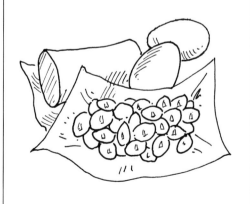

Cheese-flavored pasta

 About 15 minutes

Calories per portion: 282

For five: For the dough: 1 pound plain flour measured in the PastaMatic measuring cup - ¹/₄ cup grated Parmesan cheese. For the sauce: 2 tablespoons butter - 3 tablespoons grated Parmesan cheese.

Instructions: Pour the flour and the grated cheese into the PastaMatic bowl. Knead for 2 minutes. Add enough lukewarm water to fill the water level side for "1 pound of flour" of the measuring cup. Knead for 5 minutes. Remove the slide and extrude some dough. Turn off the PastaMatic and fasten the disc into place. Extrude and cut the pasta. Cook the pasta, reducing the cooking time by 2 minutes. Drain and serve with melted butter and grated cheese or use in soups.
Recommended shapes: conchigliette rigate, tempestina, quadrucci, assi di quadri, Ave Marie.

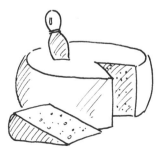

Small cheese-flavored pasta with vegetables

  About 45 minutes

Calories per portion: 340

Barbera di Langhirano (Emilia) (red)

For four: ¹/₂ pound small cheese flavored pasta - 1 leek - 1 stalk of celery - 1 carrot - 1 zucchini - ¹/₂ cup fresh spinach leaves - 2 tablespoons olive oil - 3 tablespoons butter - 9 cups broth (use stock cubes if you prefer-chicken or beef) - salt - grated Parmesan cheese.

Instructions: Wash and chop the vegetables. Heat the oil and butter in a large cooking pot and saute the vegetables for 10 minutes. Add the broth, salt and grated cheese and cook covered for 20 minutes. Add the small cheese flavored pasta when the broth reaches a boiling point, and cook a few minutes. Add more grated cheese and serve.

Fresh mushroom flavored pasta

  About 20 minutes

Calories per portion: 219

 Cortese di Gavi (Piedmont) (white)

For five: For the dough: 1 pound plain flour measured in the PastaMatic measuring cup - ¹/₄ pound fresh mushrooms - 1 egg white.
For the sauce: 2 tablespoons butter - grated Romano cheese - 1 clove garlic.

Instructions: Wash, dry and chop the mushrooms. Pour the flour and mushrooms into the PastaMatic bowl and knead for 2 minutes. Add the egg white and knead for 2 minutes. Remove the slide and extrude some dough. Turn off the PastaMatic and fasten on the disc. Cook the pasta (reduce the cooking time by 2 minutes) and drain.
Toss with the melted butter and crushed garlic and sprinkle with Romano cheese on each serving.
Recommended shapes: spaghetti, spaghettoni, chitarre.

Ham-flavored pasta

  About 15 minutes

Calories per portion: 336

Barbera di Ronciglione (Latium) aged 1 year (red)

For five: For the dough: 1 pound plain flour measured in the PastaMatic measuring cup - ¹/₄ pound lean ham - 1 egg - 1 egg yolk.
For the sauce: 2 tablespoons butter - grated Parmesan cheese.

Instructions: Chop the ham, very finely. Pour the flour and the ham into the PastaMatic bowl and knead for a few minutes. Add the eggs and knead for 6 minutes. Remove the slide and extrude some dough. Turn off the PastaMatic and fasten the disc into place. Extrude the pasta. Cook the pasta (reduce the cooking time by 2 minutes) and drain. Sprinkle with the grated cheese and toss with the melted butter.
Recommended shapes: fili d'oro, capellini, spaghetti, spaghettoni, chitarre, all kinds of tagliatelle, bucatini.

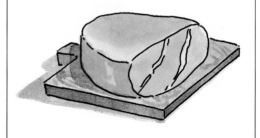

Salmon flavored pasta

About 15 minutes

Calories per portion: 275

For five: 1 pound plain flour measured in the PastaMatic measuring cup - 2 ounces smoked salmon - 3 eggs.

Instructions: Chop the salmon, very finely. Pour the flour and salmon into the PastaMatic bowl and knead for 2 minutes. Add the eggs and knead for 6 minutes. Remove the slide and allow some dough to extrude. Turn off the PastaMatic and fasten on the disc. Extrude the pasta. Cook and drain the pasta (undercook by 2 minutes). Toss with a cream or cheese sauce.
Recommended shapes: fili d'oro, capellini, spaghetti, all kinds of tagliatelle.

Tagliatelle with almond and cream sauce

About 15 minutes

Calories per portion: 280

Colli del Trasimeno bianco (Umbria) (white)

For four: 1 pound salmon flavored pasta - 2 tablespoons of butter - 3 ounces of crushed almonds - $^1/_2$ cup of cream - 2 egg yolks - $^1/_2$ grated lemon peel - salt - grated Parmesan cheese.

Instructions: Melt the butter over low heat. Mix in the crushed almonds and remove from heat. Pour the egg yolks and Parmesan cheese, cream and salt into a large mixing bowl and beat with a whisk until smooth. Cook the pasta and drain. Transfer the pasta to the mixing bowl and add the almond-butter mixture and grated lemon peel and toss through the pasta. Serve immediately.

Gorgonzola cheese flavored pasta

 About 10 minutes

Calories per portion: 346

For five: 1 pound plain flour measured in the PastaMatic measuring cup - 1 ounce of gorgonzola cheese - 2 eggs.

Instructions: Pour the flour and the crushed gorgonzola cheese into the PastaMatic bowl. Knead for a few minutes and add the eggs, using the liquid measuring cup. Knead for 6 minutes. Remove the slide and extrude some dough. Turn off the PastaMatic and fasten on the disc. Extrude the pasta. Cook the pasta (reduce the cooking time by 2 minutes) and drain. To coat the pasta, use the mozzarella and anchovy sauce or just melted butter to taste the true gorgonzola flavor.
Recommended shapes: spaghetti, spaghettoni, chitarre, all kinds of tagliatelle.

Chitarre "Viterbo style"

 About 10 minutes

Calories per portion: 527

 Rosso Piceno (Marche) (red)

For four: 1 pound gorgonzola flavored chitarre - 3 egg yolks - 4 flat anchovy fillets - 1/2 cup diced mozzarella cheese - salt and pepper - 3 tablespoons chopped parsley.

Instructions: Dice the mozzarella cheese, chop the parsley and mash the anchovies. Beat the egg yolks with salt and pepper in a large mixing bowl. Add the mozzarella and the chopped anchovies. Cook and drain the pasta and transfer to the mixing bowl and toss with the sauce. Sprinkle the chopped parsley over the pasta and toss through. Serve immediately.

Nut flavored pasta

 About 15 minutes

Calories per portion: 356

For five: 1 pound plain flour measured in the PastaMatic measuring cup - 3 ounces shelled and crushed walnuts - 3 eggs.

Instructions: Pour the flour and the walnut mixture into the PastaMatic bowl. Knead for 2 minutes. Add the eggs and knead for 6 minutes. Turn off the Pasta-Matic and fasten on the disc. Extrude the pasta. Cook the pasta (reduce the cooking time by 2 minutes) and toss with a nut sauce or melted butter.
Recommended shapes: all kinds of tagliatelle, maccheroni quadrifoglio, maccheroni, farmer's pasta.

Maccheroni Quadrifoglio with walnut sauce

 About 20 minutes

Calories per portion: 816

 Nebbiolo d'Alba (Piedmont) (red)

For four: 1 pound nut-flavored quadrifogli - 16 walnuts - ¹/₂ cup cream - 2 tablespoons butter - grated Parmesan cheese - ¹/₄ teaspoon thyme - salt and pepper - dash of cinnamon powder.

Instructions: Chop the nuts, very finely. Add the cream, salt, pepper, cinnamon powder, thyme and Parmesan cheese, and mix. Use this sauce over the nut-flavored quadrifogli. Cook and drain pasta and toss with butter, then toss the pasta with the nut sauce.

The dietician's recipes and suggestions

Introduction

According to the theories of genetic heredity, living organisms adapt themselves perfectly to the environment surrounding them and to the food available.

If that's true - and it surely is - the digestive system is (after centuries of consumption) the best thing nature has created to digest and assimilate pasta and the metabolism has come to take the greatest possible advantage from this food, by now.

We are living at a time when "skipping the first course" has turned into a widespread practice. Many diets state that pasta is fattening and, therefore, must be banned from the table for those who desire a slim figure. Haste, ignorance and brain-washing, along with all the nonsense written, make the readers try the most complicated dishes, use expensive and uncommon foods and forget the old, simple and healthy rules of traditional nutrition. Under such circumstances it is our task to state firmly that pasta is a staple of our daily diet and it is also necessary for a balanced metabolism and digestion.

If by diet we mean "balanced nutrition", our diet needs pasta.

The starch intake, provided by our "daily dish of pasta" is important for our physical well-being.

A balanced diet calls for a considerable daily intake of carbohydrates (or sugars, which include starch). The precise, necessary carbohydrates quantity is still a matter of dispute but, undoubtedly, they must exceed considerably the other nutritional elements (fats and proteins). One good source of carbohydrates is pasta, which can be dressed and eaten in a thousand different ways, therefore becoming a truly complete food.

Yet, pasta doesn't supply our body with only starch: it also gives us proteins, which, even if they have not the same biological value as animal proteins, are, nevertheless, much better than vegetable proteins. Pasta also con-

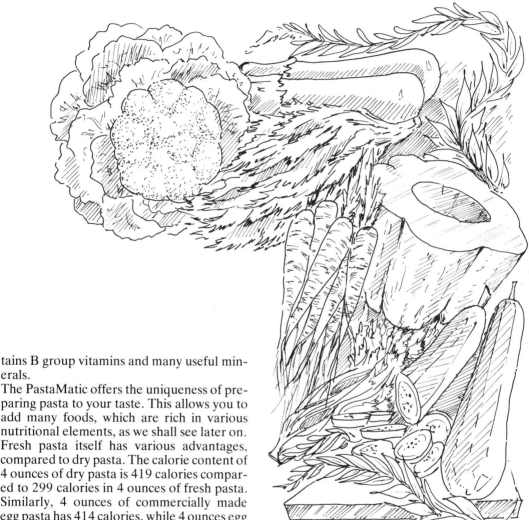

tains B group vitamins and many useful minerals.

The PastaMatic offers the uniqueness of preparing pasta to your taste. This allows you to add many foods, which are rich in various nutritional elements, as we shall see later on. Fresh pasta itself has various advantages, compared to dry pasta. The calorie content of 4 ounces of dry pasta is 419 calories compared to 299 calories in 4 ounces of fresh pasta. Similarly, 4 ounces of commercially made egg pasta has 414 calories, while 4 ounces egg pasta, prepared with the PastaMatic, supply 344 calories. Those who care for a slim figure can be reassured: it is no longer necessary to eliminate or reduce pasta dramatically. By substituting dry pasta with fresh pasta, prepared with the PastaMatic, it is possible to eat the same quantity of pasta with a remarkable saving in calories by 29%. If you prefer egg pasta, the saving will be still considerable (17%) though inferior, but that's due to the fact that egg pasta, prepared with PastaMatic, "actually" contains eggs. However, fresh pasta, made with the PastaMatic, can also be prepared to give it real nutritional properties, which can be of some help in many cases. This is what we are going to talk about in the next pages.

Pasta to suit any taste!

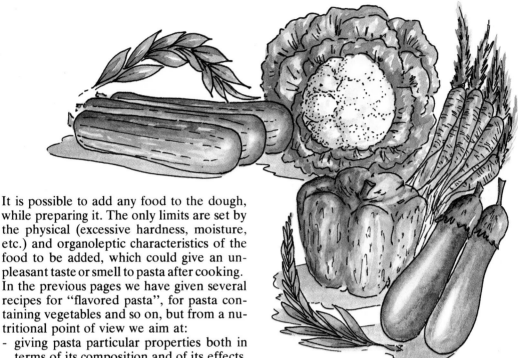

It is possible to add any food to the dough, while preparing it. The only limits are set by the physical (excessive hardness, moisture, etc.) and organoleptic characteristics of the food to be added, which could give an unpleasant taste or smell to pasta after cooking.

In the previous pages we have given several recipes for "flavored pasta", for pasta containing vegetables and so on, but from a nutritional point of view we aim at:
- giving pasta particular properties both in terms of its composition and of its effects, which could help in case of some diseases or at certain times during life;
- making all the different kinds of pasta, as appropriate as possible for every diet from a nutritional point of view. For this reason no attention has been given to egg pasta, which may not be advisable in some cases (excessive cholesterol rate, liver disorders, etc.). Furthermore, we have preferred fresh vegetable juices, obtained with BravoSimac, to whole vegetables, for people who may be suffering from colitis, for the elderly and so on. Vegetable juices are used instead of water measured accordingly in the PastaMatic liquid measuring cup. However, it is advisable not to stick too strictly to the exact cup level signs, but rather stay somewhat between the "water" and the "flour" lines in order to give pasta the right consistency and prevent it from being sticky.
(Always keep your dough in moist, walnut-sized lumps).

As in recipe n. 9 we have used baby food (veal, beef, turkey, chicken). The right way to proceed, when preparing pasta with baby food, is as follows: pour the flour into the PastaMatic bowl and, while the machine is operating, add the content of one small jar of baby food (4 ounces) for $1/2$ pound of flour or more, if you have used 1 pound of flour, through the opening of the lid. Allow to mix and knead perfectly and, then, add additional water **if necessary.**

Pasta and diseases

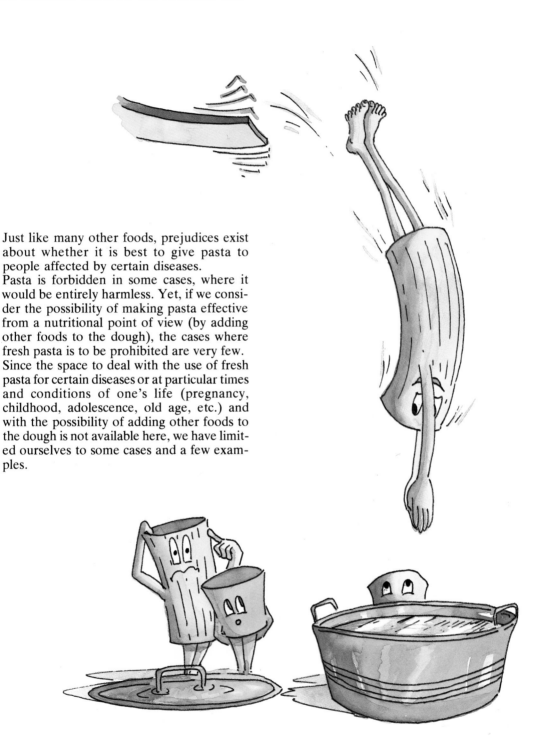

Just like many other foods, prejudices exist about whether it is best to give pasta to people affected by certain diseases.

Pasta is forbidden in some cases, where it would be entirely harmless. Yet, if we consider the possibility of making pasta effective from a nutritional point of view (by adding other foods to the dough), the cases where fresh pasta is to be prohibited are very few.

Since the space to deal with the use of fresh pasta for certain diseases or at particular times and conditions of one's life (pregnancy, childhood, adolescence, old age, etc.) and with the possibility of adding other foods to the dough is not available here, we have limited ourselves to some cases and a few examples.

OBESITY

Let's start with obesity because this is an important problem, which to some unaware people strictly bans the use of pasta. Is such a prohibition sensible? No! Undoubtedly, one needs not to eat huge quantities of pasta but to set proper amounts: we think that a daily intake of 3 ounces fresh pasta, or $3^1/_2$ ounces fresh egg pasta is a fair portion. These quantities contain respectively 225 and 297 calories; thus we do not think a dish of pasta effects a 1000 to 1200 calories daily diet. Also, pasta sauces should be kept simple, with low-fat sauces, then the additional number of calories won't be disastrous.

It is worthwhile mentioning that even a limited presence of pasta in a diet prevents, as previously stated, the constipation problem and that starch, compared to simple sugars, has the advantage of being absorbed easily, since it is a source of glucidic calories. And it is advantageous for low-calories diets, since a low absorption allows a better use of the calories.

Fresh pasta can be used in low calorie variations by adding either pulp or the juice of vegetables or fruits to the dough: celery, turnips, leeks and apples.

GAUNTNESS

After having talked about obesity, it is important to examine gauntness. It is common knowledge that gauntness is the dieticians' black sheep because even without being dangerous, it often cannot be cured despite all the most careful treatments or diets.

Nobody would ever dream to forbid the "gaunts" to eat pasta. On the contrary, they are often requested to eat it many times a day. Therefore, there is no need to recommend the use of pasta for this disorder.

Some suggestions: some vegetables and fruits act as aperitifs and are, therefore, useful to fight against the lack of appetite, which sometimes (but not always) affects gaunt people.

In case of lack of hunger, you can add some apricot, raspberry, parsley (mixed with carrot juice, recipe n° 1) or watercress juice.

To dress pasta, do not use high fat-content sauces, which are rich in calories. This will kill the appetite easily and weaken digestion. It's better to use light, tasty sauces, which can be digested easily and stimulate the appetite.

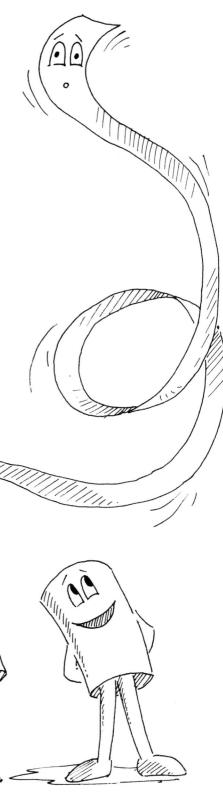

DIABETES

In case of diabetes mellitus the daily intake of carbohydrates must be strictly determined on the basis of different factors: severity and kind of diabetes, tolerance, daily insulin intake, etc. However, there is no reason why pasta could not be included in the carbohydrate intake allowed daily. It would be the dietician's task to decide the quantity.

One of the advantages offered by fresh pasta is that it allows one to determine the starch content exactly, because you know how much flour has been used to prepare the dough.

Thus it is possible to add vegetables or fruits (which can act positively against diabetes) to the dough: asparagus (recipe n° 6), cabbage (recipe n° 7), watercress, lettuce (recipe n° 8) nut, or olive juice.

HEART DISORDERS

There is no reason why pasta should be avoided in case of heart disorders (except for very severe forms, when the patient's diet must be almost liquid, to prevent even the least digestive stress). The sauces must be light, easy to digest, and the quantity of pasta allowed will be estimated according to his digestive capacity (in order to avoid overloading his stomach).

It is advisable to add some cabbage juice, which has useful, natural properties to fight against these disorders. As a matter of fact, cabbage has a diuretic action and it also act specifically against the stress of the cardiac muscle (it enlarges the coronary arteries) and it soothes the nervous system which must remain undisturbed in case of heart problems.

Many vegetables have the same action on the nervous system.

We recommend lettuce (recipe n° 8), whose juice can be used together with that of cabbage.

195

HYPERTENSION

Like heart disorders, hypertension doesn't exclude the use of pasta, no matter what the pressure level. It is necessary, in this case, to determine the quantity of pasta on the basis of the daily calorie intake allowed.

Like heart disorders, it will be considerably helpful to add cabbage juice to the dough. Other alternatives are strawberries, olives and grapes. In the case of an increase in the cholesterol level of the blood, you can also use either artichoke or nut juice.

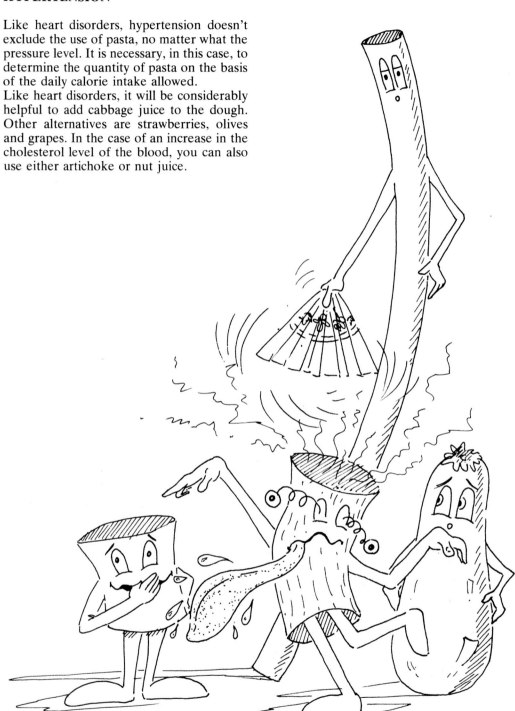

HYPOTENSION

In case of low blood pressure, pasta is highly advisable and therefore, we need not argue about the opportunity to use it or not in the presence if this disorder.

To strengthen pasta's "beneficial effect" it is useful to add to the dough the barley, that traditional medicine considers the best remedy for this disorder.

Barley is excellent and to be used either dry or after having been soaked. In the latter case, soak 1 ounce of barley in 6 cups of water and allow to boil over low heat, until the water reduces in half. You can drink the boiled juice.

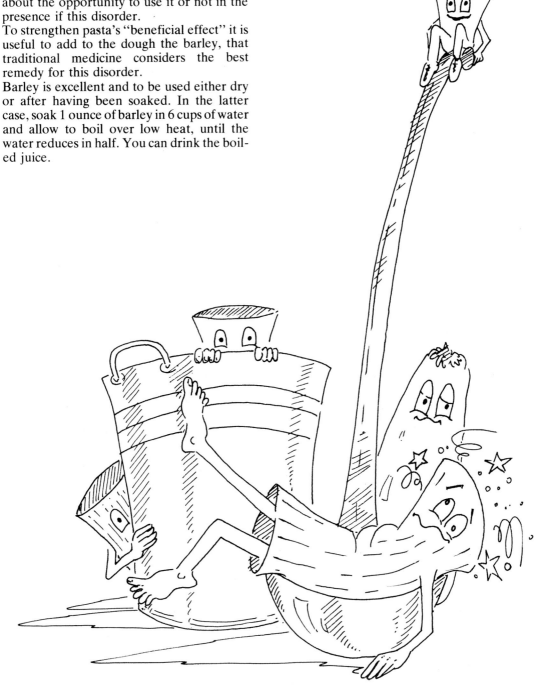

RHEUMATISM, ARTHRITIS AND UREMIA

There is no reason to prohibit pasta in case of any of these disorders. On the contrary, pasta is surely one of the most appropriate foods. You can get a specific action against these affections by adding cabbage, fennel, asparagus or lettuce juice (see recipes) individually or mixed together, to the dough.

The dressing will be chosen with extreme care; it must not contain any stimulating substances, such as pepper, paprika, etc., nor too much fat.

CONVALESCENCE AND UNDERNOURISHED

It is obvious that there is no reason to prohibit pasta in these cases. On the contrary, it must be included in the diet.

It is advisable to add to the dough vegetables because they enrich pasta with those vitamins and minerals it lacks or is provided with in small quantities only. By examining the recipes we propose at the end of this chapter, you will see that parsley and carrots increase calcium, potassium, B group vitamins, and the vitamin C content of pasta. Spinach enriches pasta remarkably with iron, vitamin B_2 and carotene (provitamin A) and so on. Thus by giving the patient pasta enriched with these vegetables, (changing vegetable every day to provide him with the full range) it is actually possible to contribute to eliminate disorders due to a lack of either minerals or vitamins and to help patient regain his strength more quickly. In particular, it is worthwhile noting that (this is extremely important for convalescent patients) pasta enriched with red pepper is by far richer in vitamin C (it acts against infections and stimulates the body) than oranges, which are the natural source of vitamin C. As a matter of fact three ounces of orange juice contains 52 milligrams of vitamin C, while 6.5 ounces of pasta enriched with three ounces of red pepper, contains 144 milligrams of vitamin C.

Pasta at particular times and ages in life

CHILDHOOD

During childhood, the human body grows and it needs nutritional foods (rich in vitamins and in proteins) but also energetic foods (rich in carbohydrates) in large quantities (due to the physical activities). Thus, pasta, in quantities according to the child's age, is highly recommended. Furthermore, since it can be dressed in a thousand different ways, it is always a "new" dish for the child, even if his appetite is poor and cannot be satisfied very easily.

Many children do not like meat and so they do not eat it very easily (causing great concerns for their mothers). In such a case, you can mix meat baby foods with the dough (recipe n° 9) then serve the pasta with a tasty sauce (any possible taste of meat will disappear completely). It's worthwhile remembering that $1/5$ ounce dried meat is equal to about 1 ounce fresh meat.

Also if you want to enrich fresh pasta with protein, you can add to the dough 1 teaspoon of a product which contains milk protein.

THE ELDERLY

The elderly's nutritional problems are not very different from the children's, even if the reasons are not the same.

Fresh pasta is useful in the elderly's diet both because (like in the children's) it can be dressed in various ways, therefore, preventing the appetite from getting weaker and also because it can be chewed quite easily. The enrichment of pasta with protein, as instructed for children, is very helpful. In fact during old age, a phenomenon, called "protein flight" occurs, due to the imperfect protein absorption, which allows a considerable quantity of unabsorbed proteins to be expelled from the body.

Subsequently, it is advisable to increase the protein content of food, just to allow the body to absorb more.

However, pasta can also be enriched with either vegetable or fruit juice with a specific action against the aging process (carrot, cabbage, see recipe, or dates).

PREGNANCY

Being an energetic food, which can be digested easily, pasta can be included in pregnant women's diet according to their digestive capacity. In this case, pasta can also be used to provide the mother's body with all the nutrients she needs in higher quantities than usual: proteins (by using either meat baby food or dairy products) minerals (by using different vegetables) vitamins (by adding either vegetables or fruits to the dough). The juice or the fruit itself such as figs, pears, apples, grapes, almonds, dates, hazelnuts, wheat, and millet, all fruits having specific actions (diuretic, restoring mineral elements, stimulating the nervous system, etc.), can be very helpful.

Recipes

1. Fresh pasta with carrot and parsley juice

Ingredients:	All-purpose flour	1/2 lb.
	carrots (extract the juice)	5 oz.
	parsley (extract the juice)	1 oz.

Content:	*Dough with flour only*		*Dough with carrots & parsley*		*Difference*
Protein	23,5	g	25,96	g	+ 10,5%
Fats	2,25	g	2,79	g	+ 24 %
Carbohydrates	182,5	g	194,8	g	+ 6,8%
Calories	872,5		933,7		+ 7 %
Calcium	35	mg	155	mg	+ 342,8%
Iron	2,5	mg	4,51	mg	+ 80,4%
Potassium	247,5	mg	852	mg	+ 244,2%
Phosphorus	220	mg	290,5	mg	+ 32,1%
Vitamin B_1	0,175	mg	0,334	mg	+ 90,8%
Vitamin B_2	0,1	mg	0,148	mg	+ 48 %
Vitamin PP	2,5	mg	3,73	mg	+ 49,2%
Carotene	0		10.788,9	μg[1]	
Vitamin C	0		51	mg	

[1] Micrograms

2. Fresh Pasta with Spinach Juice

Ingredients: All-purpose flour   1/2 lb.
                  spinach (extract the juice)   7 oz.

Content:	Dough with flour only		Dough with spinach		Difference
Protein	23,5	g	28,7	g	+ 22,1%
Fats	2,25	g	2,65	g	+ 17,8%
Carbohydrates	182,5	g	184,5	g	+ 1,1%
Calories	872,5		904,5		+ 3,7%
Calcium	35	mg	233	mg	+ 565,7%
Iron	2,5	mg	9,7	mg	+ 288 %
Potassium	247,5	mg	1309,5	mg	+ 429,1%
Phosphorus	220	mg	344	mg	+ 56,4%
Vitamin B$_1$	0,175	mg	0,335	mg	+ 91,4%
Vitamin B$_2$	0,1	mg	0,48	mg	+ 380 %
Vitamin PP	2,5	mg	3,3	mg	+ 32 %
Carotene	0		11. 300	μg^1	
Vitamin C	0		110	mg	

3. Fresh Pasta with Fennel Juice

Ingredients: All-purpose flour   1/2 lb.
                  fennels (extract the juice)   4 oz.

Content:	Dough with flour only		Dough with fennel		Difference
Protein	23,5	g	24,7	g	+ 5,1%
Fats	2,25	g	2,25	g	0 %
Carbohydrates	182,5	g	183,6	g	+ 0,5%
Calories	872,5		880,9		+ 0,9%
Calcium	35	mg	86,6	mg	+ 147,4%
Iron	2,5	mg	3,34	mg	+ 33,6%
Potassium	247,5	mg	735,9	mg	+ 197,3%
Vitamin B$_1$	0,175	mg	0,199	mg	+ 13,7%
Vitamin B$_2$	0,1	mg	0,124	mg	+ 24 %
Vitamin C	0	mg	6	mg	

4. Fresh Pasta with Red Pepper Juice

Ingredients:	All-purpose flour	1/2 lb.
	red peppers (extract the juice)	5 oz.

Content:	*Dough with flour only*		*Dough with red peppers*		*Difference*
Protein	23,5	g	24,715	g	+ 5,2%
Fats	2,25	g	2,52	g	+ 12 %
Carbohydrates	182,5	g	187,5	g	+ 2,7%
Calories	872,5		899,5		+ 3,1%
Calcium	35	mg	56,6	mg	+ 61,7%
Iron	2,5	mg	3,31	mg	+ 32,4%
Phosphorus	220	mg	282,6	mg	+ 28,5%
Vitamin B_1	0,175	mg	0,269	mg	+ 54 %
Vitamin B_2	0,1	mg	0,248	mg	+ 148,5%
Carotene	0	mg	1.607,85	μg[1]	
Vitamin C	0		232,2	mg	

5. Fresh Pasta with Zucchini Juice

Ingredients:	All-purpose flour	1/2 lb.
	zucchini (extract the juice)	1/2 lb.

Content:	*Dough with flour only*		*Dough with zucchini*		*Difference*
Protein	23,5	g	23,75	g	+ 1,1%
Fats	2,25	g	2,5	g	+ 11,1%
Carbohydrates	182,5	g	187,5	g	+ 2,7%
Calories	872,5		897,5		+ 2,9%
Calcium	35	mg	77,5	mg	+ 121,4%
Iron	2,5	mg	2,75	mg	+ 10 %
Phosphorus	220	mg	247,5	mg	+ 12,5%
Vitamin B_1	0,175	mg	0,225	mg	+ 28,6%
Vitamin B_2	0,1	mg	0,125	mg	+ 25 %
Carotene	0	mg	3.750	μg[1]	
Vitamin C	0		7,5	mg	

6. Fresh Pasta with Asparagus Juice

Ingredients:	All-purpose flour		1/2 lb.
	asparagus (extract the juice)		3 oz.

Content:	Dough with flour only		Dough with asparagus		Difference
Protein	23,5	g	26,1	g	+ 11,1%
Fats	2,25	g	2,25	g	+ 0 %
Carbohydrates	182,5	g	185,1	g	+ 1,4%
Calories	872,5		960,5		+ 10,1%
Calcium	35	mg	49	mg	+ 40 %
Iron	2,5	mg	4	mg	+ 60 %
Phosphorus	220	mg	283	mg	+ 28,6%
Vitamin B$_1$	0,175	mg	0,315	mg	+ 80 %
Vitamin B$_2$	0,1	mg	0,12	mg	+ 20 %
Vitamin PP	2,5	mg	3,8	mg	+ 52 %
Vitamin C	0		5	mg	

7. Fresh Pasta with Cabbage Juice

Ingredients:	All-purpose flour		1/2 lb.
	cabbage (extract the juice)		3 oz.

Content:	Dough with flour only		Dough with cabbage juice		Difference
Protein	23,5	g	25,1	g	+ 6,8%
Fats	2,25	g	2,35	g	+ 4,4%
Carbohydrates	182,5	g	186,9	g	+ 2,4%
Calories	872,5		896,5		+ 2,7%
Calcium	35	mg	65	mg	+ 85,7%
Iron	2,5	mg	3,2	mg	+ 28 %
Potassium	247,5	mg	535,5	mg	+ 116,3%
Phosphorus	220	mg	340	mg	+ 54,5%
Vitamin B$_1$	0,175	mg	0,215	mg	+ 22,8%
Vitamin B$_2$	0,1	mg	0,16	mg	+ 60 %
Vitamin PP	2,5	mg	3,1	mg	+ 24 %
Vitamin C	0		82	mg	

8. Fresh Pasta with Lettuce Juice

Ingredients: All-purpose flour   1/2 lb.
lettuce (extract the juice)   5 oz.

Content:	Dough with flour only		Dough with lettuce		Difference
Protein	23,5	g	26,5	g	+ 10,8%
Carbohydrates	182,5	g	185,05	g	+ 1,4%
Calories	872,5		892,9		+ 2,3%
Calcium	35	mg	120	mg	+ 242,8%
Iron	2,5	mg	4,54	mg	+ 81,6%
Potassium	247,5	mg	320,6	mg	+ 29,5%
Vitamin B_1	0,175	mg	0,277	mg	+ 58,3%
Vitamin B_2	0,1	mg	0,185	mg	+ 85 %
Vitamin PP	2,5	mg	3,69	mg	+ 47,6%
Carotene	0		287,3	μg^1	
Vitamin C	0		11,9	mg	

9. Fresh Pasta made with baby food (veal-beef-chicken or turkey)

Ingredients: All-purpose flour   1/2 lb.
baby food   4 oz.

Recipe Index

Recipes	Page	Time (in minutes)	Degree of difficulty
Maccheroni "gourmet style"	93	50	○
Maccheroni quadrati with anchovies, olives, cream	142	30	○
Maccheroni quadrati with bacon	144	40	○
Maccheroni quadrati with tomato sauce	142	25	○
Maccheroni with asparagus	145	60	○
Maccheroni with black-olive sauce-uncooked	90	30	○
Maccheroni with sausage	92	60	○
Maccheroni with tuna fish and tomatoes	93	45	○
Malloreddus with Sardinian ragu sauce	130	70	○
"Marechiaro" maccheroni	92	80	○
Mezze maniche with mushrooms	89	45	○
Mushroom pie	105	120+10	○ ○
Mushroom soup with tomato pasta	165	60	○
Nut-flavored pasta	185	15	○
Onion-flavored pasta	177	15	○
Orange-flavored pasta	170	20	○
Orecchiette with turnip-tops	124	75	○ ○
Pappardelle with duck sauce	68	120	○ ○
Pappardelle with "hare meat sauce"	68	90	○ ○
Pappardelle with mushroom sauce	66	90	○
Parmesan cheese snacks	121	40	○
Parsley-flavored pasta	178	15	○
Pasta with cocoa	166	15	○

Recipes	Page	Time (in minutes)	Degree of difficulty
Pizzoccheri	69	75	○○
Pizzoccheri with red sauce	69	80	○
Porto spaghetti sauce	42	40	○
Quadratini with broad beans soup	144	60	○
Quadrifogli with "ciociara" sauce	146	60	○
Quadrifogli with anchovies and chili	148	20	○
Quadrifogli with ricotta cheese	149	20	○
Quadrifogli with tuna fish	149	55	○
Quadrifogli with walnut sauce	185	20	○
Quadrifogli with zucchini	148	35	○
Quadrifoglietti soup, Venetian style	146	60	○
Quadrucci soup with peas	61	60	○
Quiche lorraine	104	75	○
Ravioli au gratin	154	120	○○
Ravioli with cheese	153	60+30	○○
Ravioli with zucchini	154	90+20	○○
Ricotta pie	105	120+10	○○
Rigatini with gin sauce	129	45	○
Salmon-flavored pasta	183	15	○
Salmon-flavored tagliatelle with almond and cream sauce	183	15	○
Shepherd's ravioli	155	90	○○
Short pastry tart with marmalade	106	60	○○
Small cheese-flavored pasta with vegetables	181	45	○

Recipes	Page	Time (in minutes)	Degree of difficulty
Small flat loaves with sage	101	70+10	○ ○
Small puffed strips with rosemary	97	70+10	○ ○
Small spaghetti with vegetable "Julienne" soup	43	60	○
Spaghetti "alla puttanesca"	44	30	○
Spaghetti with aubergines (eggplant) and pesto	41	40	○
Spaghetti with brandy sauce	44	55	○
Spaghetti with chicken livers	41	20	○
Spaghetti with chocolate sauce	42	15	○
Spaghetti with cuttle-fish and black liquid sauce	45	45	○ ○
Spaghetti with clam sauce	38	45	○ ○
Spaghetti with egg sauce	40	15	○
Spaghetti with olive oil and garlic	43	15	○
Spaghetti with sage	40	15	○ ○
Spaghettoni with Argentinian sauce	49	45	○
Spaghettoni with herb and ricotta cheese sauce	48	35	○
Spaghettoni with olives-Sicilian style	46	40	○
Spaghettoni with soybean sprouts	49	20	○
Spicy cookies	121	45	○
Strawberry-flavored pasta	172	20+30	○
Stuffed cheese snacks	129	50	○ ○
Sweet corn meal bread	117	50	○
Sweet ravioli with marmalade	155	30+ frying	○ ○
Tagliatelle bacon sauce	60	20	○
Tagliatelle omelette "Calabrian style" (frittata)	60	30	○ ○
Tagliatelle pie	61	90	○

Recipes	Page	Time (in minutes)	Degree of difficulty
Tagliatelle sea style	62	40	○
Tagliatelle "Spring style"	58	50	○
Tagliatelle with "harmony sauce"	58	120	○
Tagliatelle with German sauce	62	30	○
Tagliatelle with saffron and curry	65	25	○
Tarallucci	124	50	○
Tempestina with artichoke soup	45	60	○ ○
Three flavor spaghettoni	48	55	○
Tomato pasta	164	10	○
Tortellini	150	90+105	○ ○ ○
Tortellini baked in cream sauce	153	45	○
Two-color ring-shaped cakes	141	15	○
Vegetable soup	132	70	○
Whole wheat bread sticks	122	75	○ ○
Whole wheat cookies	120	40	○
Wild mushroom-flavored pasta	173	15+30	○
Zucchini pasta	168	40	○

..."Custom made" recipes with what you have in the kitchen...

Index

Printed in Italy
by SAGDOS
Officine Grafiche e Legatoria S.p.A.
Brugherio (Milano)